IT'S A BABY BOY!

*The Unique Wonder and
Special Nature of Your Son
from Pregnancy to Two Years*

The Gurian Institute

Stacie Bering, MD, and
Adie Goldberg, ACSW, MEd

FOREWORD BY MICHAEL GURIAN

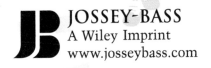

JOSSEY-BASS
A Wiley Imprint
www.josseybass.com

Published by Jossey-Bass
A Wiley Imprint
989 Market Street, San Francisco, CA 94103-1741—www.josseybass.com

Library of Congress Cataloging-in-Publication Data

Bering, Stacie, date.
  It's a baby boy! : the unique wonder and special nature of your son from pregnancy to two years / Stacie Bering and Adie Goldberg ; foreword by Michael Gurian.
    p. cm.
  Includes bibliographical references and index.
  ISBN 978-0-470-24338-1 (pbk.)
  1. Infant boys—Development. 2. Infant boys—Care. 3. Infants—Development. 4. Toddlers—Development. 5. Boys. I. Goldberg, Adie, date. II. Title. III. Title: It is a baby boy.
  HQ774.B444 2009
  305.232081—dc22

2008031672

Printed in the United States of America
FIRST EDITION
PB Printing   10 9 8 7 6 5 4 3 2 1

Contents

Foreword

Congratulations! You have a brand new baby boy!

Having a baby boy will change your lives in beautiful ways that you could not have imagined until now. With your new baby boy in your arms, your home, your relationships, and your day-to-day existence will flower as they never have before. To have such a child is to experience ecstatic joy and humbling awe at the miracles inherent in the universe.

As with every great event in our lives, however, having a new baby boy presents challenges. Before you had your son, people may have smiled, "Life will never be the same!" Now here you are—life will never be the same . . . and a little help would be nice!

If you have received or picked up this book, you might be wondering:

How does one care for a baby boy in particular?

What does this young son need?

- What are key developmental moments in his life?
- What are accurate expectations for his development?
- How are his needs the same as any child, and yet, also, unique to him as an individual boy?

All of us at the Gurian Institute are devoted to providing science-based and life-affirming answers to parents' questions about how to raise their children. In this book, you'll find information, wisdom, stories, and fascinating science about your developing boy.

Dr. Stacie Bering, an obstetrician who specializes in women's health and child development, and Adie Goldberg, a clinical social worker who specializes in early childhood education, have culled through the best new literature (and best old wisdom) on raising boys in order to bring you this book. They have also infused this book with their own personal experience with patients. Between them, Dr. Bering and Ms. Goldberg have sixty years' experience in helping families of young children.

Along with their experience and understanding, Dr. Bering and Ms. Goldberg are also Certified Gurian Institute Trainers. Thus they specialize in helping parents understand the individual needs of *boys* and *girls*. Boys and girls are similar, but they are also different. I hope as you read this book, you'll be intrigued by how wonderfully similar and different they are.

Enjoy this book and enjoy your beautiful boy. If you can, share comments with us on www.gurianinstitute.com. We look forward to hearing about how your son is flourishing. The world needs his passion and purpose, and I know he will make you proud!

—Michael Gurian, president, the Gurian Institute

From generation to generation.
To Jeffry, Cassie, and Zack,
Emily, Maggie, Chloe, and Robb,
and
the families who have entrusted their stories to us.

Acknowledgments

Baby boys grow best when there are more than their two loving parents involved in their care. Families thrive in a circle of support. This is the case when it comes to writing books as well.

Michael Gurian is at the core of the professional circle of this book. Last summer the phone rang and it was Michael. He said he had an opportunity. When Michael calls with an opportunity there is usually growth and a fair bit of work involved. Writing this book and its companion book for girls was just such an opportunity. Michael has a passion for making sure that boys, girls, and their parents are supported and informed as they embark on the parenting journey. We cannot begin to thank Michael for the advice, inspiration, and guidance he has freely given us. His generosity has not gone unnoticed.

However, vision alone does not sustain the writing of a book. Alan Rinzler, our editor at Jossey-Bass, assisted by his editorial team of Carol Hartland, Nana Twumasi, and Donna Cohn, moved us and the project forward with his editorial expertise. He has been more than patient with a pair of first-time authors. We have learned much under his tutelage and we can truly say that we are stronger writers at the conclusion of this project.

Over twenty years ago we began working together at Woman-Health, an OB-GYN clinic. Women came to us to share their concerns, fears, and dreams for and about their children. We offered advice despite the fact that we were still without children of our own. Five children later, we are wiser and humbled. We offer a special thank-you to the patients of WomanHealth who shared their lives with us. The staff at WomanHealth were patient with us over countless lunches. Their good humor sustained us, and their stories have made us both laugh and cry.

Pam Silverstein was the founding physician of WomanHealth. Her husband, Steve, and their children, Shayna and Josh, completed our families' circle of support. We both cherish their wisdom, love, and loyalty especially during this writing process.

Please indulge us for a moment as we acknowledge our own families, for they have taught us more than all the collected years of postgraduate education between us. Stacie would like to thank Jeffry Finer, without whom she would never have known the joy of parenthood, and her two children, Cassie and Zachary, who, even as young adults, continue to guide her in this on-the-job training that is the true nature of being a parent.

Adie would like to thank Robb for his computer knowledge, patience with the writing process, and his ability to still make her laugh at the end of the day. To her daughters, Emily and Maggie, who listened *ad nauseam* long distance, gave feedback on early drafts, and asked questions that continue to make their mother think, a mother's thank-you and love. A special thank-you to Chloe, who, as the last of the littermates still at home, was asked to be the most patient with us as we wrote this book. She served as our memory bank, reminding us of stories long forgotten.

Our thank-you to each of our readers. You will continue to teach us and remind us that there is always much to learn.

Stacie Bering, MD
Adie Goldberg, ACSW, MEd

IT'S A BABY BOY!

Introduction:
It's a Baby Boy!

Congratulations! Your father is beaming. "It's a boy!" he tells his buddies at the senior center where he leads a group for new grandfathers.

You and your husband, Sam, already have one healthy daughter, born eight years ago. It wasn't until the moment of her birth that you found out your baby was a Clara and not a Clarence. Now, at thirty-five, pregnant again, your doctor ordered an amniocentesis that was performed at week sixteen of your pregnancy due to "advanced maternal age" (a phrase you detest). He explained that mothers over the age of thirty-five are at increased risk for carrying a child with Down syndrome or other rare chromosomal abnormalities.

Your doctor also asked if you wanted to know the sex of your baby. You do, but Sam doesn't want to be told the results. He's already sure you are having a boy. He also reminds you how thrilling it was to hear the nurse midwife's dramatic announcement of Clara's arrival. But your curiosity is getting the better of you.

Like good married partners, you reach a compromise. You will get the results including gender, but hard as it will be, you won't tell Sam unless and until he asks. At week eighteen, you've just received the word. You are having a healthy baby boy, with no signs of any chromosomal problems! You remain very careful to talk about "the baby" and never refer to him as "he" or "him." Then, at week twenty, Sam can't stand it any longer and receives confirmation for what he has known all along. He is having a son.

If you didn't have an amnio, you might have discovered your baby's gender at an eighteen-week ultrasound. Your doctor or midwife will often order a routine ultrasound during your second trimester to make sure that your baby is developing normally and that your due date is accurate. During this office procedure, the technician, called an ultrasonographer, carefully examines your baby's anatomy and while you may not identify everything you see on the screen, you'll usually recognize the tiny unmistakable genitals between HIS legs.

Then again, perhaps you found out the old-fashioned way, seconds after giving birth, still gasping for breath, as your doctor proclaimed, "It's a boy!"

Whatever way you hear the news, welcome to the exciting world of having a baby boy!

Since the birth of your new son, it may be that well-meaning family and friends have been full of special advice about boys. This advice may range from the strange and mysterious to the clichés of conventional wisdom. You may have heard:

"A boy needs to be swaddled in soft linen because his skin is more sensitive!"

"A boy needs to be bundled up tightly in a scratchy burlap bag to roughen up his skin."

"You must not circumcise. It's barbaric, it ruins him for life."

"No, you must circumcise, for cleanliness and for preventing disease!"

You'll hear that your boy will be harder to raise than a girl; or that he'll be easier. You'll hear he'll be more independent and rebellious than a girl, or that because he's more straightforward and on the surface, he'll be easier to read than your more complex and sophisticated young girl.

Baby Boy Story

Ellen says her son just came out different. Suzie, her firstborn, made every object a playmate and sat quietly in Ellen's lap during her building's co-op nursery meetings, studying the faces of the other mothers around her. Ellen acknowledges, "I was spoiled. Then my son Jacob came along and every object wasn't a playmate, it was a projectile. Every toy fork or spoon or piece of food in the house became a car or a weapon!"

Whatever the message, most of your family, friends, and other "experts" in your life will tell you that your baby boy is different from a girl, because, as everyone knows in their heart of hearts, "boys will be boys."

Boys Really Are Different from Girls

The latest research, using the most up-to-date technological hardware for scanning brains while the body acts, has shown us what role the gender of a brain plays in impacting human behavior. We have solid evidence that your son's brain structure, genetic predisposition, and hormonal development all play a critical role in shaping your man-to-be. We also have sound evidence that boys' brains are different and develop differently from girls' brains starting a few weeks after conception.

Functional Magnetic Resonance Imaging (fMRI for short) provides detailed images showing which areas of the brain are activated during various activities and events. These studies show how your son uses his brain differently than his sister. What's even more interesting is that if we took a slice of your boy's brain we wouldn't be able to tell his race, ethnicity, or religion.

We could, however, confirm that the brain belonged to a boy.

Here's what else we know about the differences between baby boys and baby girls at birth:

• Your son at birth is larger than the girl lying in the layette next to him in the nursery.

• His blue-capped head is 12–20 percent larger than the pink-capped head of his neighbor. His hat will need to stretch to accommodate his larger head circumference.

• He has more cells of gray matter inside that cap than a female does. Gray matter contains fibers that block the spreading of information in his brain. This is what gives men their ability to focus intently on work. Remember that the majority of chess grandmasters are male even if your boy doesn't hear you call his name while he plays video games.

• Your son will use his male brain structure in a different way than a female uses her brain structure. The male brain tends to use either one hemisphere or the other and relies on specialized brain regions when performing a task. A female spreads the task across the hemispheres of her brain.

• Your son may not experience as much pain and discomfort as a newborn baby girl. If someone drops a metal pan in the nursery, a baby girl may cry out in irritation. If, however, your son does get

● **BABY BOY BRAIN FACT** ●
What Is the Y Chromosome Effect?

Some would say it's a man's world, but it doesn't start that way *in utero*. This difference is due to the genetic makeup of boys and girls. Two Xs are, at least in the womb and at birth, better than one. The X chromosome carries immunity factors, and the female infants' chances of survival are increased by having two X chromosomes. If there's a problem with one, they have an alternative to draw from. Since males have one Y chromosome and only one X chromosome, there is no fallback.

Take a breath and relax, however, since the vast majority of male pregnancies end with the birth of a beautiful, healthy baby boy.

disturbed, he'll need firmer patting and louder comfort sounds than the gentle touch that soothes that fussy girl.

• Yet, at birth your guy is actually the weaker of the two sexes. In the womb, boys tend to be more vulnerable to maternal stress and more predisposed to such difficulties as premature births, congenital malformations, and respiratory difficulties.

Even though there are more boys conceived than girls, it's an uphill battle for those male fetuses. The male fetus is more likely to suffer almost all the catastrophes that can happen before birth—miscarriage, respiratory distress, and infections. Premature birth and stillbirth are more common in boys, and during birth the boy's brain is more vulnerable to damage, and thus by birth he is on average days or even weeks behind his sister developmentally.

Baby Boy Story

Sandy, a thirty-four-year-old yoga instructor and certified massage therapist, came directly from the neonatal intensive care unit to her obstetrician's office. She was crying and confused. She wondered aloud what she had done wrong? Her son Maddox had been born ten weeks prematurely, and even though he was progressing nicely, Sandy still blamed herself.

Sandy had done nothing wrong and had, in fact, been a model patient. Fit when she became pregnant, she continued to exercise, eat healthy foods and follow through with the prenatal care visits set by her obstetrician.

How This Book Works

We hope this book will help you be the best parent possible to your baby son as he starts out in the world. We don't intend this book to be the last word on all the details of baby care. We want you to know what is special and unique about having a baby boy. Each chapter contains boxes that include real-life "Baby Boy Stories" and "Baby Boy Brain Facts," with the latest in scientific information and professional advice.

Chapter One will guide you through the biology of your pregnancy. You will discover how DNA and hormones interact to shape a boy's development. We'll try to demystify the secret drama of human chromosomes, genes, and brain development that unfolds *in utero*. In addition to looking at how your son is developing, we'll update you on the most recent research regarding nutrition, the effects of hyper-stimulating the fetus, the impact of stress, the use of alcohol, drugs, and nicotine, and the role of exercise during pregnancy.

Chapter Two begins with a quick review of how biology and environment work together during the first year of your son's life. Every sensory experience your newborn has is shaping the way his brain circuits are being wired. Each time your son has a new experience, he is creating new connections in his brain. Your boy is building on the wiring he created while still inside of you. Each experience, like an electrical signal, passes on a message. The more experiences, the more repetition, and eventually neural roads form. Through this process, learning takes place and his brain becomes "hardwired."

For years, folks have debated the role of nurture versus nature in the shaping of a newborn. Many favored the importance of nurturing, arguing that people are molded by the outside influences on their brains. The pressure can be overwhelming for parents who struggle with the potential power of this type of influence. Advances in brain research and neuroscience, however, have given us evidence that your son's brain has its own nature, that it's programmed by genes and evolution to function in a certain way, and that much of this will happen no matter what environmental influences you bring to bear.

Joyce, a grandmother and nurse with three grandsons and two granddaughters, understands this. One day she exclaimed to the other nurses in her clinic's lunchroom, "I don't know what it is about my boys. All my grandsons were born making car noises. How do they know how to do that?" She added, laughing, "Of course it's easy to figure out what to get them for birthdays."

Chapter Two concludes with brain-building activities for your boy, parenting tips for you, a summary of developmental highlights, and a final note for mothers.

● **BABY BOY BRAIN FACT** ●

A Hands-On Kinda Guy

Whereas females, on average, use more of their cerebral cortex for words and emotions, your boy will most likely use more of his cortex for spatial and mechanical functioning. This will affect how your boy will best learn. Some boys benefit from more hands-on activities.

The brain chemistry that was set in motion and described in the first two chapters doesn't end there. Chapter Three looks at what lies ahead for your son and what you and your partner can do to facilitate your boy's development through his preschool years.

Why are boys as a group more aggressive than girls? Why do they tend to prefer physical play? The first section of Chapter Three focuses on the full range of boys' play, toys, and friendships. Not all boys turn every stick into a gun. Your son might be just as content turning the pages of his board book. We'll help you identify what is the range of normal, what skills your son will need to play, as well as clarify the difference between vigorous play and violence.

The final section of Chapter Three presents a preview of several developmental milestones you will face in the next few years, such as toilet training and school. Parents and experts weigh in on how to pick a preschool or day-care provider and on the specific learning needs of boys during these preschool years.

Finally, Chapter Four will help you realize that you are not alone. This chapter helps you identify and locate your sources of support. Sometimes we need to be reminded that our relationships with our partner, extended family, and ourselves need as much care and understanding during this time as our little guy does.

Gendered brains and chemistry don't stop at childhood. This chapter ends with a look at how mothers and fathers parent differently. We'll let biology explain why it seems that babies' fathers might sleep through their son's nighttime crying while mothers may not. Parents have lots to tell and we'll let you in on their successes and advice.

We hope this book helps you both enjoy your baby boy and appreciate the incredible ride ahead! And we promise that no matter what your gender, parenting your boy will make you laugh more, cry more, and love more than you ever have before.

The Boy
Inside You

Amber, a labor and delivery nurse, lay in the ultrasound suite, gazing at the monitor as her baby danced across the screen. Pregnant with her second child at thirty-eight, her records included the phrase "advanced maternal age." Thus, unlike her pregnancy four years earlier, she elected to have this amniocentesis to check for chromosomal abnormalities.

The sonographer moved the machine's wand over Amber's abdomen, looking at her baby's brain, heart, and other internal body parts.

Amber was gazing at the machine's monitor when an unmistakable image floated by. "Do you want to know what sex the baby is?" the sonographer asked.

"I think I already do!" Amber replied.

Together, the two women watched in amusement. Amber's baby lay, legs open, an undisputable appendage lying between them. Every time the sonographer moved her wand, the baby moved too, making sure his legs were spread open, giving the women yet another good view.

"He was determined to make sure we knew he was a BOY," Amber laughed two years later. "I think he was giving me fair warning for all those times he was going to laugh at me as he ran naked through the house tugging on his penis!"

Perhaps, like Amber, you have had an amnio and received the word you were having a healthy boy. Then again, you might already have had two girls and were secretly hoping for a boy this third time

● BABY BOY BRAIN FACT ●
Why Does a Doctor Suggest an Amniocentesis?

- You're thirty-five or older and the risk of Down syndrome and other, rarer, chromosomal abnormalities, increases with age. Down syndrome is the result of a baby having an extra chromosome.
- You had a blood test called a triple or quadruple screen at week sixteen of your pregnancy and the results were abnormal. With an abnormal result you are at increased risk for delivering a child with Down syndrome, a spinal defect (spina bifida), or a severe brain abnormality. REMEMBER! It is quite common to have a false positive result. Usually it comes from you or your doctor miscalculating your due date. An amnio and an ultrasound will give you a more accurate result.
- You had an ultrasound, and something abnormal was detected.
- You have a history of a chromosomal abnormality in your family.
- You have already delivered a child with a chromosomal abnormality.

around when you got a good peek at your sixteen-week ultrasound. You know it's a boy in there. You might have decided to wait until your baby was born to find out if you were carrying a boy or a girl. You responded to the curiosity of well-meaning coworkers "Do you want a boy or a girl?" with the response, "Either, as long as it's healthy."

Perhaps you're already holding that baby boy in your arms as you turn the pages of this chapter, trying to remember what it felt like to have your sleeping boy stretch or hiccup inside of you. Some couples might wonder if it's possible to choose the sex of their baby. They ask if there are any methods that increase the chances of having a boy. Science has come back with a resounding "NO!"

● BABY BOY BRAIN FACT ●

Guaranteeing a Boy: Should We Make Love Standing Up?

Depending on the myth, you should

- Eat more salty foods, red meat, fish, eggs, chicken, pickles, olives, peas, corn, figs, apricots, raisins, prunes, beans, avocado, zucchini, mushrooms, and lots of beans of all kinds
- Eat less milk and dairy
- Have your (male) partner drink a strong cup of coffee one-half hour before retiring to the bedroom
- Make love standing up, at night, on the day of ovulation, or on odd days of the month
- Make sure the woman has her orgasm first
- Put your legs up in the air for an hour after making love
- Douche before making love

Remember:

- All of these suggestions are myths, not based in reality.
- None of these suggestions has held up to scientific scrutiny.
- But most statistics are on your side. Fifty-one boys are born for every fifty girls.

However you made your boy, you're about to find out about how genes, DNA, and chromosomes worked together to create him, how the powerful male hormone testosterone furthers his development, and what scientists are learning about what makes your baby boy so different from your best friend's daughter, starting from the moment of conception.

If you're curious to know why your friends and family are telling you that boys are so different from girls, read on!

Gene Talk

1. What is DNA? The body is made up of different kinds of cells: liver cells, skin cells, and blood cells to name a few. DNA is every cell's set of instructions or blueprint. It tells the cell whether it's going to help your little boy hear or help his heart beat.

2. What are genes, anyway? Genes are made up of the DNA. They are the instruction manual for your boy's body. They tell his body how to develop and function. Genes determine whether your boy will grow tall and slender like Aunt Debbie or short and squat like Uncle Harry. Your son's genes determine whether he'll have a cholesterol problem and a tendency toward heart disease. Your son has an estimated twenty-five thousand genes.

3. What's a chromosome and where can you find one? In the center of most of your body's cells, you'll find the nucleus, or the cell's command center. Within that nucleus are the chromosomes, the gene holders of your body. Chromosomes come in pairs, like shoes. We each have twenty-three pairs. When you and your partner created your son, you each gave him half of the set of twenty-three chromosomes.

4. What makes my boy a boy? Blame it on the chromosomes, specifically two called X and Y, and they couldn't be more different. Mom's egg always passes on an X chromosome and Dad's sperm can pass on either an X or Y chromosome. In your case, it was a Y! Human boys are XY.

● **BABY BOY BRAIN FACT** ●
A Lot of Neural Mileage

Your son's forty-six chromosomes contain so much information that if you wrote it all down, the data would fill a stack of books two hundred feet high! If you pulled the entire twisted DNA from a single cell and stretched it out, it would be as long as a car. If you stretched out all the DNA in a human body, it would stretch to the sun and back six hundred times!

Although Mom's X chromosome is long and lean, containing up to fourteen hundred genes, Dad's stubby Y chromosome contains only about four hundred. It is the smallest chromosome in your boy's body. Unlike all the other chromosomes, it has no mate. Although the Y chromosome is kind of puny compared to the X chromosome, it has a very important gene called SRY. Think of it as the sex spot on the Y chromosome. Some researchers call this the testes-determining region, which gives you a hint of how important it is to the developing male embryo. It is also known as a *master gene,* because the work it does motivates other genes on other chromosomes to get involved in making your boy's boy parts.

Together, these genes direct the formation of a boy. Now his journey begins.

From Embryo to Baby Boy

Your boy's journey to being a male took place in three stages, starting with the development of his testicles. Next came his internal organs and finally the rest of his external genitals made their appearance.

Step 1: Formation of his testicles. About week eight of your pregnancy, the SRY gene kicked in and directed the formation of your son's testicles, which began to produce testosterone. By this time your boy, only a tiny embryo, was bathed in the male hormone. This was the first of three "hits" of testosterone. The first one lasts until the twenty-fourth week of your pregnancy.

Step 2: Formation of his internal male organs. Now testosterone takes over as director of the show. A pair of scene-stealing cords appear in your son's abdomen, called the Wolffian ducts. They turned into your son's internal genital structures. There was another set of cords, the Mullerian ducts, also auditioning for the role, and had they gotten the part, they would have become female internal anatomy. But no, a product of the Y chromosome performed a disappearing act on the Mullerian ducts, so that the boy structures took center stage.

Step 3: His external boy parts. Up until nine to ten weeks' gestation, the external genital area was rather nondescript. There was nothing to let you know that this was a boy or a girl. But testosterone steps up again and produces DHT, which begins to run the show. Up until this point, there was nothing more than a bump between your son's legs. Thanks to DHT, this bump became his penis and the area below this bump formed an empty scrotum. Eventually, the testicles, which are at this point up inside the abdomen, will assume their rightful place inside your son's scrotum.

Testosterone Hits, Hits, and Hits Again

Boys experience three series of "hits" of testosterone during their lives.

The first series, as we just described, came when the testicles began pouring out the testosterone that led to the formation of your baby's boy parts. The second occurs shortly after birth and the third hit occurs with puberty.

That first series of testosterone hits directed the development of the structures that will later be necessary for reproduction. We know less about the effects of the second series of hits. We think they help in getting the structures ready for your boy to make babies of his own. Right now this must seem like eons from now!

The final series of hits at puberty will set the processes in motion that will change your boy into an adult male. When puberty hits, you will hardly recognize your boy as he sprouts up, bulks out, and his voice lowers an octave or two. The androgens (testosterone and its buddies) are working on his muscles and bones, spurring on their growth. Although it's hard to imagine now, your boy child will begin to grow pubic, underarm, facial, and body hair, all directed by the same testosterone that made this embryo declare his boy status. Testosterone is not only responsible for the physical changes your son will experience, but also unleashes a stream of decidedly male behaviors.

Is Your Boy's Brain Different from His Sister's?

Yes. Absolutely.

Testosterone is responsible for the obvious physical differences we see in boys and girls, men and women. The latest research suggests that the Y chromosome and testosterone and its buddies have profound effects on the formation of your boy's brain. These changes begin while your son's brain and nervous system are forming *in utero*.

Just as in the genital system, if you could peer in on early brain development, you couldn't tell the difference between a boy and girl brain. We all start out the same. But even before you missed your period, your son's nervous system was beginning on its male journey.

How Does Your Baby Boy's Brain Grow?

You have just taken an early pregnancy test and gotten the news. Already your son's brain had started to form. Your baby was little more than a tiny flat disk floating over a ball of cells. The transformation of this fertilized blob of chemically driven cells into a young man who will solve complex problems, build interesting structures, and read history textbooks is an amazing process.

A tiny groove developed along the length of this disk. The groove deepened and eventually sealed its edges over to form a long tube, the neural tube. By five weeks, the organ that looked like a lumpy inchworm had already embarked on the most spectacular feat of human development: the creation of the deeply creased cerebral cortex, the part of the brain that eventually allows your son to move, think, speak, plan, and create. The brain of your growing boy changes so much over the next thirty-four weeks that researchers are able to tell you how many weeks pregnant you are by looking at your son's brain.

What's Unique About a Baby Boy's Brain?

Your son's brain will perform millions of tasks in a uniquely male way.

Starting at eight weeks, his brain is flooded with multiple hits of male hormones. Traveling via the bloodstream from the testicles to the brain, testosterone and its relatives modify brain function and shape how the brain processes, stores, and retrieves information. Testosterone actually affects how your boy's brain circuitry is laid down. Through a complicated interplay of genes and sex hormones, your baby's brain will take on the structure and function of a male brain.

His brain will

- Control his body temperature, blood pressure, heart rate, and breathing
- Translate a flood of information about the world around him from his eyes, ears, nose, and taste buds
- Regulate his physical motion when walking, talking, standing, or sitting
- Think, dream, reason, and experience emotions

And this is all done by an organ that is about the size of a small grapefruit!

A Quick Tour of the Baby Boy Brain

The key players in your son's brain are

1. The cerebrum. The biggest part of the brain is the cerebrum, also called the cerebral hemispheres. Most of the brain's weight, 85 percent, is devoted to the cerebrum. The cerebrum is the seat of higher brain functions—thinking, reasoning, speaking, and interpreting the environment. Memories are stored here, and emotions processed. When your son starts to crawl, his cerebrum will tell his arms and legs what to do.

2. Cerebellum. Next in the lineup is the cerebellum, which is at the back of the brain, below the cerebrum. Although a lot smaller than the cerebrum, about one-eighth of its size, the cerebellum is a very important part of the brain. It controls balance, movement, and coordination (how the muscles work together). Because of the cerebellum, your son will be able to stand upright, keep his balance, walk, run, and jump.

3. Brain stem. Another small but mighty brain part is the brain stem, which sits beneath the cerebrum, in front of the cerebellum. The brain stem connects the brain to the spinal cord and is in charge of all the basic functions your boy's body needs to stay alive—breathing air, digesting food, and circulating blood.

4. Pituitary gland. The pea-sized, powerful pituitary gland is in charge of making your boy grow large by producing and releasing growth hormones into his body.

5. Hypothalamus. Last, but certainly not least, is the hypothalamus, the brain's regulator of emotions, body temperature, and food and water intake. At some point your son will tell you to stop putting a coat on him because YOU are cold—and you can thank his hypothalamus for that!

How Does a Tube Turn into a Brain?

The neural tube (the sealed-off set of early cells) starts to imitate a pretzel by swelling, folding, and contorting to form the various parts of the brain. It divides into the forebrain, midbrain, and hindbrain. Your little guy's eyes and nose will develop from the division of the neural tube that became the forebrain. This area also develops into the cerebrum and the hypothalamus. The midbrain is destined to become the brainstem. The hindbrain will become the cerebellum. You son's brain is growing rapidly at this point. If you were able to look in on him now, you would be struck by how odd he looks. He's almost all head!

Inside the tube, the cells divide rapidly and cause the tube to thicken. Some of these cells become neurons or nerve cells. Neurons are initially produced in the central canal of the neural tube. Although they are born there, they don't stay put, as they migrate to their final destination in the brain. These cells collect together to form the different centers of the brain and spinal cord, and they send out axons, long, threadlike extensions that connect with other nerves.

At nine weeks, the embryo's ballooning brain allows your boy to bend his body, hiccup, and react to loud sounds.

By week ten, your boy's brain is producing almost 250,000 new neurons every minute.

By your second trimester the grooves and furrows of your son's brain begin developing. Nature has taken advantage of these peaks and valleys to cram as many neurons as possible into a relatively small space.

By forty weeks, or term, his brain is an engineering masterpiece designed by genes and hormones.

Is Your "Boy Pregnancy" Different from a "Girl Pregnancy"?

Yes, but you're not likely to notice. Here's what researchers have found:

- Boy fetuses are in general more active than girl fetuses.
- Feeling hungry? Women pregnant with boys eat about ten percent more calories that those carrying girls. The good news is that you won't be gaining any more weight with a boy pregnancy! This research explains why those baby boys weigh more. A signal from your male fetus tells you he has higher energy needs than a girl.

- At each week of pregnancy, boys weigh more than girls, so that when they're born, boys weigh on average a half pound more than girls. Their heads are larger, and they're longer than the girls.

● BABY BOY BRAIN FACT ●
The Old Wives Weigh In

Here's some wisdom from a time-honored source—"The Old Wives"—and they say you're carrying a boy if

- Your baby's heart rate is less than 140 beats per minute.
- You're carrying the baby out front.
- You're carrying the baby low.
- The hair on your legs is growing faster.
- Your hands are rough.
- You crave salt.
- Your complexion improves.

We're still learning what makes boy pregnancies different from girl pregnancies. It's an active area of research, so stay tuned!

Will My Boy Be Okay? Ten Simple Things to Do

Now that you're pregnant, you're probably paying closer attention to your diet. Getting the right nutrients is not only important for your little one's health—it can affect his intelligence too. Certain foods positively affect your boy's memory and capacity to learn, and others can hinder proper brain development. These smart moves will help you maximize your future Einstein's learning.

1. First of all, strive to gain the right amount of weight. Obstetricians recommend that women of normal weight gain between twenty-five and thirty-five pounds during their pregnancy. A study from the National Institutes of Health found that women who follow that prescription have children with higher IQs than kids born to moms who gained more or less weight during their pregnancy. This is sort of a domino effect, as your prenatal weight gain affects your baby's birth weight, which, in turn, affects his brain size and IQ. Gaining too much or too little weight during pregnancy can lead to birth complications that can affect your baby. Women who are over- or underweight should check with their OB or midwife to find out their recommended weight gain.

2. Get those vitamins and minerals.

- Without enough **iron**, important areas of your baby's brain won't grow as they should, and this could lead to permanent damage. Red meat, beans, fortified cereals, and spinach are wonderful sources of iron.
- **Folic acid** is critical for the proper development of the neural tube. Eat some leafy green vegetables, such as kale and spinach. Dried beans and orange juice are also good sources. Fortunately, most breads, cereals, and grain products are fortified with extra folic acid.
- There's new evidence linking adequate **calcium** intake to a decreased risk of severe toxemia—a pregnancy complication that can result in preterm delivery and improper fetal growth.
- **Take your prenatal vitamins—even when you can't stomach the food!** It's often hard for a pregnant woman to take in all the nutrients she needs, especially during the first trimester of pregnancy, when the smell or taste

of any food might send her to the toilet bowl rather than the kitchen table.

The prenatal vitamins your doctor or midwife recommends are specially formulated for pregnancy. And before you ditch your vitamins because they make you sick, try taking them with food, or change brands.

Remember, prenatal vitamins are meant to supplement a well-balanced diet. They are not meant to replace the nutrients you need, merely add to them. Prenatal vitamins don't contain all the calcium and iron you need, for example.

3. Make sure you visit your dentist regularly. Women with gum disease are more likely than those with good gum health to deliver their babies prematurely. Some studies suggest that the risk may be up to nine times higher! And being premature is not good for your baby boy's brain. Your natural incubator, your uterus, is better for him than any high-tech machine in the neonatal intensive care unit.

4. Get your thyroid tested. Many women have an underactive thyroid gland that often goes undetected. A simple blood test can let you know whether you need to take a thyroid supplement, which can easily correct the problem. Children born to mothers with untreated thyroid disease during pregnancy score lower on IQ tests than children born to healthy moms.

5. Bump up your choline. The nutrient you never heard of is critical for your son's normal brain development. Studies in animals indicate that choline plays a crucial role in the construction of two major brain centers for learning and memory. A diet low in choline during pregnancy can permanently harm your baby boy's brain chemistry and development. Moms-to-be need 450 milligrams of the nutrient each day. That's easy if your diet includes eggs, beef, and dairy products. Soybeans are also a good source.

6. Eat fish, an excellent food, but certain fish can have high concentrations of mercury and should be avoided. Don't eat shark, swordfish, or king mackerel. Mercury can affect your son's brain development, and not in a good way. But fish, rich in omega-3 fatty acids, may boost your baby's brainpower.

● **BABY BOY BRAIN FACT** ●

You Really Are What You Eat

So is your little boy. In a study from Harvard Medical School, the more fish women ate during the second trimester, the higher their babies scored on a mental development test at six months of age.

7. Pump up the protein. Proteins are your boy's first set of building blocks. They help him grow from a single fertilized cell to a cuddly bundle. That's an awful lot of work for a little guy, and he needs your help.

8. Stay away from alcohol. Alcohol is not good for developing babies. Alcohol passes directly through the placenta to your baby, and your baby's blood alcohol level will be about the same as yours. So if you're feeling tipsy, so is he. Alcohol can not only lead to brain damage, it can also lower your son's testosterone levels. The most dangerous time seems to be during the mid second trimester, coinciding with the first series of testosterone hits, but no time is definitely safe.

9. Give up the cigarettes while you're at it, and avoid illegal drugs. We know that boys are already at higher risk for a preterm delivery, and babies whose mothers smoke are at even greater risk for being born prematurely. A smoking mother's placenta is smaller and doesn't work as well. Cigarette smoking actually raises testosterone levels in your fetus! Research indicates that the extra exposure to testosterone can result in an abnormally aggressive boy prone to attention-deficit/hyperactivity disorder (ADHD).

10. Get your body moving. It's good for you and may help boost your son's brainpower. There's evidence that at five years of age, children born to mothers who exercised while pregnant performed significantly better on general intelligence and oral language tests. The vibrations or sounds exercise causes *in utero* may have boosted neurological development. Not to mention exercise helps keep your weight gain under control!

● BABY BOY BRAIN FACT ●
Mom's Stress

Maternal stress hormones may inhibit a fetus's brain growth by restricting blood flow to the uterus. Another theory is that certain brain chemicals are released in high levels during stressful moments. These chemicals can interfere with the production of brain neurons and synapses. We all have occasional bad days, but if you are continually feeling overwhelmed by responsibilities, depressed, or angry, give yourself permission to get help. It's OK to seek professional assistance for problems you can't resolve with the help of family or friends.

What Else Can I Do for My Baby's Brain?

Various authors and "experts" have suggested hyper-stimulating your baby at regular intervals to assist in his brain development. Suggestions include speaking to him through a paper tube, playing Mozart, reading to him in a foreign language, or shooting flashing lights at the mother's abdomen.

Does such stimulation work? There are numerous testimonials in advertisements supporting these methods. Users swear that their children are smarter, more physically coordinated and socially adept than average. Scientists, however, are skeptical. There is no way to really test how a baby would turn out with and without this stimulation.

No one can say for certain when a fetus is awake, so interfering with jabs to the abdomen may be interfering with his natural sleep patterns. It seems counterintuitive to wake a sleeping newborn baby. Why would you do such a thing *in utero*?

Gently talking to your baby, however, seems to pose little risk and in fact may help you as much as your baby. Thinking about your boy, talking to him, having your spouse talk to him, will all help to prepare you for this new boy who's going to jump into your life and turn it and himself upside down.

● BABY BOY BRAIN FACT ●
The Role of Music

Listening to a soothing sonata is a great way to relax during pregnancy, but it won't make your baby any smarter. There is no evidence that playing classical CDs or foreign language tapes will boost your boy's brain power, either before birth or after.

By now we hope you have a pretty good idea how genetics and hormones have combined to shape the baby boy in your womb or in your arms. Next, we'll give you a preview of what to expect of that boy and his brain this coming year and what you and your partner can do to nurture the nature of this baby boy.

His First Year

Your boy has arrived home, his brain in tow.

While you're exhausted with middle-of-the-night feeding, diaper changes, laundry, and just trying to find some time to brush your teeth, it seems all your little guy does is eat, sleep, and poop. Wondering how someone so small can demand so much of your time and attention, you might not notice that behind your son's seemingly simple existence an awe-inspiring process is taking place. Believe it or not, you're not the only one working hard!

● BABY BOY BRAIN FACT ●
Faster Than a Speeding Bullet

In the first month of life, your son's brain will lay down three million neuron-to-neuron connections per second!

You now know your son came home with a male-biased brain. His XY blueprint was created at the moment of conception. Testosterone hits *in utero* played a major role in developing his male brain.

As your baby grows, his biological blueprint is directing his maturation process. The basic wiring will be fine-tuned by experience. As your boy responds to his environment—big sisters, the dog, your apartment, your backyard, whatever it might be—his brain will react by creating yet more circuitry, expanding on his boy wiring. Exactly how his brain structure affects who your son will become is the subject of continued dialogue. What is clear is that there *are* differences between boys and girls, and the gendered brain cannot be remolded. Your son will often behave differently from his sister or female cousin.

Your son's brain will shape the way he sees, hears, smells, and tastes. Nerves run from his eyes, ears, nose, and tongue to his brain, and this decidedly male brain will interpret all this data.

As an exhausted parent of a newborn, you may not be tuned into the many behavioral differences between your son and a newborn girl. At first, most of the differences are obvious only to researchers. But if you are the parents of a boy-girl twins, you'll be more attuned to many of those distinctions as you watch your babies grow up side by side.

The ways of boys are often completely foreign to their mothers—you may not understand your son's anatomy and activity level or his emotional makeup. As for dads, it's been quite a while since your own days in the crib and just because your guy has an immature version of your anatomy, he may not be a junior you. Your boy might be an alien creature for both of you, especially if you were raised in a house with sisters, doll houses, and tea parties.

Emily, the mother of two boys, Ethan and Caleb, ages two and four, and eight-year-old Hannah, observed that her boys never built fairy villages like their older sister. She also knew that if they ever found one, they'd stomp on it just like they would any bug they

● **BABY BOY BRAIN FACT** ●

You Say Po-tay-to and I Say Po-tah-to

Using PET scans and fMRIs, researchers have already detected one hundred structural differences between the male and female brain.

found. As a preschooler, Hannah carefully escorted each bug she'd encounter to the side of the walk before resuming her play. Ethan and Caleb, however, energetically begin performing "the squishy," a bug-pulverizing, stomping dance.

Emily was right on the mark when she observed how different her boys are from their sister. From the beginning both Ethan and Caleb were interested in motion and objects. Their sister was attuned to faces and smiles. Emily's three children did have something in common, however. They all began to experience and make sense of the world starting with their brains—sort of a physiological trickle-down effect that eventually worked its way to their feet.

What is going on inside that bald head you caress first thing each morning and (if you're lucky) only a few times during the night?

Baby Boy Story

Sandy, mother of nine-month-old Nowell, invited their neighbors and their little girl, Ariella, over for a play date. Nowell had spent the morning crawling around on the grassy lawn and eating dirt as he picked up rocks from the flower bed. He greeted the visitors with a dirty face and a muddy baby mustache, the knees of his pants grimy with lawn crud. Ariella, four months older than Nowell, was five pounds lighter. She tiptoed around on delicate feet and sniffed at the yellow dandelion flowers.

Sandy remembered sitting on the lawn with her neighbors, observing their children, her boy and this dainty young woman-to-be. They were a study in differences. She thought to herself that she had never told Nowell that eating dirt was more fun than smelling a flower.

This first year is a physical sensation roller coaster, both for you and your son. From the very beginning, he'll experience his world through all his senses—touch, sight, sound, smell, and taste—as a male person.

How Your Boy Experiences Sight

For this first year, your son will be experiencing the world through his senses; the more experiences you give him, the more his senses will mature. Observers in the newborn nursery have found that even at one day old, boys were more interested in looking at an object (the moving mobile over their bassinet) than girls, who preferred live human faces.

At birth your son can see, but he can only focus on objects eight to twelve inches away. He may actually be just as comfortable staring at objects as he is looking at your face.

How Does Your Baby Boy See?

- By six weeks, he can focus at a distance of one to two feet.
- By four months, he can see objects, close or far, about as well as an adult.
- By six months, he'll see as well as he ever will.

As early as two to four days after birth, researchers have observed a difference in how long your boy will stare at you versus the amount of time a girl will spend staring at her parents. On average, boys will spend half as much time making eye contact. And by four months, that same girl will be able to distinguish pictures of people she knows from people she doesn't.

Your boy in all likelihood will be less able to do that but more inclined to stare at that rotating mobile than gaze into your eyes. It's hard not to take his roaming eye personally, even if he is just a few months old!

How Does the Eye Work?

- Light traveling into the eye focuses at the back of the eyeball, on the retina.
- There are specialized cells in the retina, rods and cones, that detect light.
- The rods and cones are attached to nerves that collect together in the optic nerve. That nerve sends the information to the visual center of the brain.
- Rods record a scene like a black-and-white TV set. They tell your boy the shape of things, and detect movement. They are very sensitive to light, and can "see" objects in very dim light (such as at nighttime), but not in color. Each human eye has about 120 million rods.
- Cones are responsible for color and fine detail. Each cone is sensitive to one of three colors—green, red, or blue. Cones only work in bright light, which is why you can't see colors at night. Each eye has about six million cones.
- Cells in the retina are primed to take in sex hormones, which means that eyes develop differently in boys and girls. Remember those testosterone hits? Studies suggest that male retinas are better at detecting motion (think rods), but female retinas are better at seeing color and texture (the cones). This means that your boy may be visually attracted to things that move. In a study of one-year-olds, researchers found that boys preferred watching films of cars but girls preferred films of people's faces.

Baby Boy Story

Lacey and Harry had just had their son and were house hunting for something with more space. Bringing eight-month-old Andy along with them, they visited a home with a large playroom, equipped with cars and blocks as well as dolls and a pretend kitchen. While talking with their realtor, Harry put Andy down. Lacey laughs as she describes the beeline Andy made, crawling straight for the cars.

Helping Your Boy Develop Sight

Make eye contact. Take advantage of those moments when your boy's eyes are open and focused on you. Look right into them. Each time he stares at you, he's building memory.

Let him reflect. Have your baby stare at himself in the mirror. At first, he may think he's just eyeing another cute kid, but he'll love making the "other" baby wave his arms and smile.

Share the view. Take your baby in his sling or baby carrier on walks. Facing in, he will share you; facing out, he will share your view.

How Your Boy Experiences Sound

Your boy has been listening to the muffled sounds of your world since the end of your second trimester. If Milo, your family dog, barked at the garbagemen, your son heard an *in utero* version of that barking. If his older brothers stormed into the house letting the back door slam behind them as they yelled across the kitchen, he heard that, too.

Once born, your little guy does not have the same ability to distinguish sounds as his female counterparts. As early as one week of

● BABY BOY BRAIN FACT ●
Hearing Sensitivity

In a study of 350 newborn baby boys and girls, researchers found that most boys were less sensitive to sound than girls, especially sounds at higher frequencies.

age, researchers have documented that boys hear differently from girls. A female newborn can distinguish the cry of another baby from the general background noise, but most likely your son will not be able to. Baby girls respond twice as frequently to loud sounds as boys.

The age-old parenting strategy of soothing a fussy boy by playing and vigorously patting him on the back but soothing a fussy girl by softly cooing and humming may have its origins not in social stereotyping but in Mom's innate understanding of biology.

How Does Your Baby Boy Hear?

• The outer ear, the part you can see and that you carefully bathe, collects sound and funnels it inward to the eardrum.

• When sound hits the eardrum, it causes three tiny bones in the middle ear to vibrate.

• These bones transfer their vibrations to the cochlea, the snail-shaped hearing organ in the inner ear. The cochlea is filled with fluid that moves with vibrations. This stimulates tiny hairs that are part of the cochlea.

• When the hair cells are stimulated, they generate nerve impulses that are sent along the auditory nerve to the temporal lobe, the part of the brain that is the hearing, speech, and memory center.

We have known for years that boys do not, on average, hear as well as girls and that girls show this superiority from birth on.

Baby Boy Story

Zeke's family had been friends with Mary's since their first Lamaze class. Seventy-two hours after Zeke was born, Mary made her appearance. Their families spent time together every week, eating dinner and comparing parenting notes. One evening Zeke's parents arrived at Mary's house. Squirming to get down, Zeke crawled directly to the fireplace. Mary was fast on his heels. While playing there, Zeke tried to pull himself upright on the stand that held the fireplace tools. Stand and tools came clattering down. Startled, Mary dissolved instantly into loud sobs while Zeke crawled into the fireplace, digging happily in the ashes.

Recently, technology has been able to give us a hint as to why this is. Boys are born with a longer and more flexible cochlea. This difference makes it more difficult for a boy's hearing organ to respond as sensitively as a girl's.

● **BABY BOY BRAIN FACT** ●

His Sound-Locating Skill

Even though research gives infant girls the edge in hearing, your infant boy is already better able to identify where a sound originates. Researchers argue this skill had evolutionary significance because it gave men the ability to locate the direction of an oncoming threat. Although your son won't be looking out for a charging woolly mammoth, he will use this skill to find out where the noisemaking toy is in the playroom or point out from which direction the fire engine is approaching.

Helping Your Boy Develop Hearing

Blab away. You may get a blank look, but go ahead and speak. Leave short pauses where your boy would respond. Some researchers attribute part of a boy's lagging language skills to the hearing differences between boys and girls. Keep talking. He will catch on to your rhythm and will in time fill in the silent spaces.

Activate his auditory wiring. Brain connections are built and strengthened when we use them. The more you repeat sounds, such as "moooooo" or "vrooooom," the more your boy's faint neural connections are fortified. Your son's auditory synapses will multiply steadily from nine months to two years.

Don't rely on TV and videos. Your boy's brain learns best by interacting—hands-on, or in this case, "ears-on." Having music on in the background and handing your boy noisy rattles or a wooden spoon and pot is much more interactive than turning on an educational video.

How Your Boy Experiences Smell and Taste

The world smells and tastes differently to your son than it does to a newborn girl. The smell and taste area in our brains is located in the limbic system, which is the seat of memory and emotions. We all remember the scent of something special like a lilac bush sending us back to the backyard of our childhood home. Sensory programming is quite powerful and begins at birth. Your boy's nose plays an important role in his emotional development.

Smell is the most advanced of all the senses at birth. The nose is your son's main organ of taste as well as smell. The so-called taste buds on your son's tongue can only distinguish four qualities—

sweet, sour, bitter, and salty—all other tastes are detected by the smell receptors high up in his nasal passages.

Your boy has been smelling and tasting throughout gestation. Inhaling and swallowing your amniotic fluid, his smelling receptors were bathed in sensation.

The sense of smell is extremely important in your boy's life. Until he can see better, his perception of the world is that which is found in his vicinity and it is perceived best through his nose.

How Does Your Baby Boy's Sense of Smell Work?

- The smell sensor, the olfactory epithelium, is located up in the nose. In your nose it would be about three inches from your nostrils.

- Smells in the form of chemical molecules enter the nose, dissolve in his mucus, and stimulate cells in the smell sensors. These cells connect with the olfactory nerve, which sends nerve impulses to his brain

- Your boy has about forty million smell receptors in his nose.

 ### Baby Boy Story

Debra, a junior high science teacher, observed that her infant son Pete was as incapable of distinguishing what smelled good from what smelled stinky as were her eighth-grade male students. Pete barely looked up from play, even with a poopy diaper. Her junior high boys were equally oblivious to the smells emanating from their bodies. She joked that in both cases she was the one who noticed when it was time for showers and deodorant, or a diaper change and good-smelling baby lotion.

Although research tells us that newborns can respond within the first few hours of life to the smell of their mother's breast, this skill has actually only been observed in girls and not in newborn boys. Your boy's testosterone is responsible for decreasing his smell sensitivity. Despite that decreased sensitivity, your scent will be special to him, helping him forge a bond that is essential for his survival.

How Does Your Baby Boy's Sense of Taste Work?

- Chemicals from food dissolve in saliva and bathe the taste buds on your son's tongue.
- Each taste bud has 50 to 150 receptors that respond best to one of the four basic tastes—sweet, salty, sour, and bitter.
- Just as with his sense of smell, nerve impulses go out to his brain, to the cerebral cortex and to the limbic system.
- Seventy-five percent of what your boy perceives as taste actually comes from the sense of smell. That's why, when your baby has a cold, he can't taste much and isn't always interested in food!

Helping Your Boy Develop Taste

Breast-feed, breast-feed, breast-feed. Yes, you're tired. It would be so nice to have your husband take over one night and let you sleep. But if you've never tasted breast milk, it really is yummy. Yes, there are drawbacks to breast-feeding (lack of sleep is probably coming to your mind at this moment!). We'd be remiss, however, if we did not note that research keeps uncovering reasons why breast milk remains the best. There are many wonderful books on infant nutrition and breast-feeding. These books discuss how some mothers deal with being on call 24/7 by pumping milk to be used in bottles given by Dad or a caregiver or by supplementing breast milk with formula. Ask your pediatrician to recommend a favorite book on infant nutrition.

Give your guy lots of variety. When it's time to introduce solid foods, remember food and its textures are a chance for exploration and discovery.

But what if you can't breast-feed? There are reasons you may find yourself unable to breast-feed. Perhaps you have a medical condition or are taking medicine that can be harmful to your infant. Perhaps your son is a gnawer rather than a sucker, and despite consultation with a lactation expert, breast-feeding has become a tense and agonizing experience for you and your child. Or perhaps you are an adopting parent.

Whatever the reason, our advice is to relax and go easy on yourself. There are excellent formulas available. Ask your pediatrician which might be best for your baby. A definite advantage to bottle-feeding is being able to share the mealtime responsibilities with your partner. And you'll be able to know exactly how much your baby is getting each time he chows down.

How Your Boy Experiences Touch

Skin is the largest organ of your boy's body. From birth, the girls in the nursery are far more sensitive to physical sensations than your son is. Changes in temperature and a wet diaper won't upset most guys nearly as much. Research has found that the most sensitive boy in the nursery is less sensitive to touch than the least sensitive female. He literally has thicker skin!

How Does Your Baby Boy's Sense of Touch Work?

- Touch sensors reside in the bottom layer of his skin, called the dermis.

- Your baby's skin has about twenty different kinds of sensors that send information through his spinal cord to his brain. The most common sensors are those responsible for detecting heat, cold, pain, and pressure.

- Your son has more pain receptors than any other kind. That's a good thing, because pain receptors protect him from harm. Before his brain registers the fact that he's just touched a hot stove, his brain stem makes sure that he pulls his hand away!

Baby Boy Story

Sara couldn't get over the difference between her daughter Reyna, her firstborn, and her new baby boy, Nathan. Reyna would fuss if her clothes didn't feel right. She would shriek if her socks weren't put on just so, with the toe seam up. Yet when Nathan came home from day care, full of good cheer, Sarah would find his socks bunched up in the toes of his boots. "He was totally oblivious!" Sara laughed.

Helping That Thick-Skinned Fella to Feel

Get touchy-feely. Keep a box of differently textured fabrics for your baby and run them over his naked belly.

Don't be afraid to roughhouse. Your boy is comfortable with much more tactile stimulation than you realize. Don't panic when your husband insists on throwing him up in the air!

How Does Your Boy Learn to Speak?

It really is true, as most parents report, that boys often use fewer words and talk later than girls. For many of you, this may be the first time you actually observe real differences between your son's development and the development of your friends' daughter. Genes really do play a role in verbal skills. On average, boys will talk later than girls, use fewer words, and talk in shorter sentences than the female toddlers in his age group.

By midway next year, your boy may have about forty words, fifty fewer than the ninety that make up a toddler girls' vocabulary.

Boys and girls use their brains differently when it comes to language. Technology lets us peek into the working brain and allows us to see these differences. Research is just beginning to shed some real light on what is going on in male and female brains that sets the stage for these differences. There is a striking difference between how males and females use the hemispheres of their brains,

Baby Boy Story

Leslie, the mother of twenty-month-old Martin, was concerned that her son did not jabber when riding in his car seat in the same way her firstborn daughter Kim did. Driving along the freeway, Kim would give her mother a travel narrative, "Tree!" "Pretty!" "Mama!" "Baby!" And so they would drive along. Martin reserved his limited vocabulary for the moment they would drive past the car wrecking yard, acres and acres of smashed cars in various states of disrepair. Then he would shout out, "Mine! Mine! Mine!"

particularly the left one. Boys rely heavily on their left hemisphere, but girls tend to share the load more equally between left and right. Your boy will rely heavily on Broca's area, the language area in the left hemisphere of his brain When researchers measured the size of the *planum temporale,* a language area in both hemispheres of the male and female brains, they found that females devoted an equal amount of space in both hemispheres to it, but males tipped the scales to the left.

● **BABY BOY BRAIN FACT** ●

Extra Language Neurons

All the brain circuitry for language is ready and waiting at birth for your son to start communicating with you, but the wires haven't all been connected. By birth, his genes created a basic map for language acquisition. Your boy has more neurons than he'll need for language acquisition, and by year's end he'll begin pruning away those he didn't use. Your baby boy was born with all the basic wiring necessary to speak any language in the world.

For the first two years of his life, your boy's dynamic brain will experience the world by listening to you. Neurons will fire. Sounds and patterns are repeated and those same neurons will fire again and again. Every time you see a train and repeat, "chug a chug a, choo, choo," it sets the stage for the day when your boy sees the train and pipes up, "Choo choo!" This is how connections are strengthened. Neuroscientists quip, "The neurons that fire together, wire together."

Had researchers been able to peek in on your boy's brain on his first day of life, they would have been able to observe the differences between his brain circuitry and the girl born in the birthing suite next door. Even then his neurons were responding to the excited speech around him in different areas of his brain than she did in hers. By three months, the scan shows us that he is responding in his left hemisphere while the girl is using her right. She was born with a larger language area in the left hemisphere and had a head start on that side. Hearing differences play a role in your son's language development. Nerve impulses from the right ear go primarily to the left side of the brain, and vice versa. In one experiment, researchers put earphones on male and female children and played sounds to either the right or left ear. If we did this to your son, we might find him to be more likely to respond better and retain more of what he heard in his right ear.

Other imaging results show us that the language centers known as Broca's and Wernicke's areas are proportionately larger in females than in males—more neurons, denser packing, longer dendrites. It's no wonder your boy on average will use far fewer words each day than the average girl's.

As if all these brain differences weren't enough cause for boys to lag in language development, researchers have found that even though boys and girls follow similar patterns of growth and development both *in utero* and beyond, there are measurable differences in when the upper airways and oral motor pathways develop in boys versus girls. Again it is the girls with the head start.

So what can the parent of a boy do?

First, don't worry! Just scan the fiction section of your local bookstore and you'll see volumes of books written by men. Boys do a major catch-up in language skills at around age four or five, although standardized tests continue to show a male-female gap persisting throughout high school.

In the meantime however:

Pump up the volume. No need for the soft coos. Go gaga! You're likely to be rewarded with a deep baby boy belly laugh when your guy tunes into your antics.

Get in the habit of reading to your son over and over. Babies as young as eight months old can recognize sequences in stories read to them repeatedly. Make your son the hero of your stories.

Give him one-on-one support. Your boy may need more opportunity to pick up language than girls. If your son is in day care make sure his caregivers give him the time he needs.

Sing a song. Learn as many baby tunes as you can. Make up your own verses. Use rhymes. Again repetition helps your boy learn. Reciting rhymes provides opportunities for boys to use a lot of language unconsciously. No surprise, but rowdy rhymes and songs with animal noises and sounds that go "bang" and "boom" are big hits!

Limit the TV and video time. Babies learn words from people, not videos. Researchers find the babies who were taught a word face to face rather than while watching a video were better able to match the word with its object.

Don't hold yourself responsible for the differences between your son's language development and your niece's. Some argue that we talk more to girls because they are more socially engaging. But in fact, researchers find that the amount of time you'll spend talking to your son early in life doesn't differ from the amount of time you spent talking to his older sister.

Your Little Man in Motion

This first year your boy will learn how to move and use his body. Initially, his movements are simply the uncontrolled, reflexive movements he was born with. Over time, he'll learn to move his body parts voluntarily and the majority of boys reach those developmental milestones before baby girls of the same age. He might be able to lift his head sooner, crawl sooner, stand with support sooner, and walk sooner.

● **BABY BOY BRAIN FACT** ●

A Plan for His Movement

In general, babies begin developing motor skills from the center of the body outward and from head to tail. Your son will learn to control his head and neck before maneuvering his arms. Then he'll learn to maneuver his arms before manipulating his fingers.

Ask most mothers and they'll tell you that many boys are active from the beginning. Eileen, a patient at a birthing center, pregnant with her second son, remarked that from the moment she could feel her first son growing inside her, he moved *all day!*

"He's three now and to this day," she notes, "he still moves all day long. In his sleep or during play time, he is constantly moving!"

Research agrees! Male infants are often more active than females and use more space being active. This finding doesn't change over time. If anything, the difference in activity levels between the sexes only increases as they grow. With this difference comes boys' increased exploration of bigger spaces and his greater comfort with distance from you!

More on Movement: How Does He Touch His Nose?

It's not that simple!

The brain controls all of the body's voluntary movements. Your son's motor cortex, located in the rear part of his frontal lobe, is the brain area most involved in controlling your son's voluntary movements.

Your son's motor cortex receives pieces of information from other areas of the brain. He needs to know where his body is; he needs to remember he wants to touch his nose; and then he needs

---

Baby Boy Story

John, a nursing student, has two boys, three years and eleven months old. Fascinated by his younger son's behavior, he shared with us how his little guy, Marty, uses him as a human jungle gym. Marty is at that stage where he walks a few steps, plops down, crawls a few feet, and stands up again to walk a few more steps. Wherever Marty is in the room, he makes his way over to Dad, who might be sitting in a chair or on the couch. Once there, he stands up, bumps (purposely) into Daddy and climbs up and over John's legs before he continues toddling along.

Already a problem solver at one year, Marty finds his older brother to be an acceptable alternative climbing apparatus if Dad isn't around. It doesn't matter who is his jungle gym. The little guy is enjoying the body contact and the challenge of figuring out how to coordinate his body movements to get around, up, or over his favorite human obstacles.

---

to develop an appropriate strategy for attaining his goal—moving his hand. Each of these tasks is directed from different areas of his brain. To deploy his body parts smoothly, he needs an internal control center that can precisely regulate the sequence and duration of his movements. That control center is the cerebellum.

Baby Boy Story

Harry and Beth now have three grown boys. Beth was attending a baby shower for a "second time" mother. Each of the attendees was asked to give a piece of advice to the guest of honor. Beth reminded her that even though she might be having a second boy, not to count on them being similar. She told the story of her first two boys.

Her oldest son, Aaron, was a late walker, content to scoot around until seventeen months and willing to let Beth or Harry carry him. Anthony, her second son, was a completely different boy. One day Beth turned around to see thirteen-month-old Anthony up from his nap, in the kitchen, not wearing anything but a diaper. She asked Harry why he hadn't dressed Anthony. But Harry hadn't brought Anthony into the kitchen, nor had he woken him from his nap. It was then they realized they needed to do something different about Anthony's crib. Their boy had gotten himself up from his nap, out of the crib, and had taken off his clothes before toddling into the kitchen.

Your son will most likely be able to coordinate his motor brain functions earlier than a girl the same age. He may on average start walking earlier than she and may outperform her in running and jumping. Researchers think this may be related to his stronger visual-spatial relation skills (something we'll address in greater detail next chapter). Despite these skills, the parts of the brain responsible for fine motor skills will mature more slowly for most boys. Your son may be able to leap tall buildings but he will have greater difficulty holding a pencil or picking up his Cheerios.

Remember, your boy will develop at his own pace. He may be crawling before the other boys in your playgroup. Then again he may remain on all fours while those same boys are cruising around on two small feet. Even though there are differences between genders in how development unfolds, there is also a lot of variation within gender. Right now, motor milestones are the most obvious measure for parents of what's going on inside their son's brain. It's the rare mom or dad that doesn't feel secretly proud or disappointed as they compare their son's motor skills to the skills of the other babies in his age group.

Boy Play for Motor Development

Is it possible to encourage your son's motor development? Check this out.

Babyproof. Allow your boy play that is safe and unrestricted. He needs space to move.

Babyproof again. As your boy goes from crawling to walking to climbing, he'll find new things to explore and more ways to get himself into trouble. He doesn't want to hear "no" at every turn, and you don't want to say it.

Don't make it too easy, give him challenges. Unlike infant girls who are more likely to dissolve into tears when frustrated, your boy will learn better when there are low levels of stress to propel him on.

Be patient. Repetition isn't boring for your boy!

Take time. Yes, it's easier and more efficient to keep your son in the stroller or back pack than to chase him down the grocery aisles or spend three minutes staring at the bug on the sidewalk, only to take two steps and then find a rock that needs to be kicked back in the opposite direction! But let him take his time and explore. If he could, he'd thank you for not rushing him along.

Your Son and His Penis

When your son discovers his hands for the first time, turning them over and over, waving them in front of his eyes and clutching them, it is a developmental milestone worthy of a note in the baby book. For most mothers, however, penis discovery is a bit more baffling and not usually treated as worthy of such official documentation.

Infant Boy Erections

It is normal for your son to explore his body and his penis will certainly inspire his infant curiosity. He'll reach for his penis every chance he gets, especially when you want to diaper or bathe him. This is a battle you can't win. To many mothers' dismay and to your boy's delight he will get infant-size erections. Mothers are confused. Do I stop him? Don't I?

These erections are normal. You can expect your little guy to have them several times a day, and as every man knows, this will continue on into adulthood. Often his tiny erection will be in response to a full bladder, so if you happen to see the erection while changing his diaper, you may want to shield his penis with a diaper or a cloth to avoid getting a warm stream in your eye!

Just as your son discovered the joys of grabbing his feet, he will soon discover that grabbing his penis feels good. By the time he is a toddler, he's likely to figure out that penis tugging feels better than toe tugging, so he's likely to do it a lot. This isn't masturbation; it's exploration. And for some children, this behavior can be self-soothing, much like thumb-sucking. If he gets a little carried away, this is the time to talk to him about what's appropriate to do in privacy and what's for all the world to see.

Whether or not your son can stimulate himself to orgasm is speculation. Ejaculation, however, won't happen until he is near puberty, when his third series of testosterone hits.

To Circumcise or Not

As a parent of a boy you'll have many penis questions.

The first question most parents confront is whether to circumcise or not. This is a decision you will be asked to make while at the hospital.

There are many social, cultural, and religious arguments pro and con. You may be feeling pressure to circumcise or not to from family, friends, or the media. The debate over the medical value of circumcision continues. On the one hand, the American Academy of Pediatrics (AAP), although acknowledging that potential medical benefits exist, does not recommend routine circumcision.

On the other hand, studies show that circumcised boys have fewer bladder and kidney infections, are less likely to become infected with HIV and some other sexually transmitted diseases, and are dramatically less likely to get cancer of the penis (a very rare form of cancer).

The practice of newborn circumcision, although not medically necessary, is a safe procedure with few risks, most of them minor.

The AAP recognizes there are many factors playing a role in your decision regarding circumcision:

- **Religion.** For Jews, circumcision is both a religious obligation and a cultural tradition. Muslims also practice circumcision, although it is not viewed as a commandment from the prophet.
- **Tradition.** If the baby's father is circumcised, he may want his son to be as well, fearing that one day his son may ask why their penises look different. As the vast majority of men in the United States are circumcised, this factor often plays a big role in parents' decision making.
- **Hygiene.** Proper cleaning of the uncircumcised penis involves pulling back the foreskin and gently cleaning the head of the penis. Some parents worry that their son might neglect to clean his penis thoroughly.

Some anti-circumcision groups claim that sex is better for both the man and woman when the man is uncircumcised. It's hard to imagine how one could prove this! Sexuality is much more than the joining of a penis (circumcised or not) and a vagina.

As with any surgery, ask your doctor to discuss with you the risks and benefits of the procedure before you make your decision.

Hygiene

Cleaning a penis? Most first-time boy mothers are concerned that they might hurt their son. Experienced moms will reassure you that removing those persistent bits of lint and fluff stuck to your son's penis isn't a painful experience, and will tell you that once your boy is able to sit up in his bath, his penis will become one of his favorite tub toys.

Baby Boy Story

At a lunchroom table, Suzy, a mother of three girls, asked the other mothers at the table, "When do baby boys discover their penises?" The table erupted with laughter as all the mothers of boys had stories to tell.

Diane asserted that Ethan had discovered his penis by day two. She went on to talk about how a few years later, she found Ethan, now a preschooler, in his bedroom with Jason, his eighteen-month-old brother. Neither of them had their pants on. They were pulling on their penises and stretching out their scrotums. As calmly as possible, she gently asked the boys what they were doing. Ethan looked back at her and answered, "We're pretending we're flying squirrels. Wanna play?"

Diane declined.

A Few Final Words for Moms

Mothers and fathers interact differently with their sons. Moms tend to restrain and soothe their little guys, perfect for a tired boy but not so good for a fella who's ready to move. Dads tend to roughhouse with their boys. They're loud. They pedal their boys' little legs, hang them upside down, poke them, and in general, provide opportunities for action. This is a good balance for a boy who can flourish with two such types of interaction.

Remember Emily, mom to Caleb, Ethan, and Hannah? Now that they are getting older, her boys need less and less of Emily's softness and want more and more activity. Her daughter's most rambunctious girlfriends rarely expressed their energy in the boisterous ways of her boys. In the next few years, both you and Emily will be learning more about body noises, vehicle sounds, and wrestling than you had ever imagined.

We'll be talking about all that physical play in the next chapter. But don't worry. Your son will always need that special relationship with you. He'll still walk around your bed in the middle of the night, bypassing his dad, because it's you he'll want to soothe him after that bad dream he just had.

Gazing into the Future: Toddler and Preschool Boys

If you are like most parents, you won't remember much of your son's first year. The details of first smiles, first steps, and first words are fuzzy, lost in the blur of sleepless nights and busy, over-scheduled days. By the end of that first year, however, you will have figured out the feeding and diapering routines. You'll be coming up for air just in time to witness a magical transformation—your boy changing from a helpless and dependent baby to a moving, talking, and remembering toddler. He'll be busy; he'll be curious; he'll be a little man in motion.

With your boy changing at breakneck speed, how will you keep up? This chapter will walk you or, more appropriately, run you though a review of boys' motor, language, cognitive, emotional, and social development during their toddler and preschool years. We'll also give

● BABY BOY BRAIN FACT ●
The Exuberant Brain

At birth, your son had all the neurons he'll ever need in his cerebral cortex. But they weren't very well connected to one another. In the first two years of life, connections between nerve cells will sprout out in a massive burst. At times, your boy will be making these connections at an astonishing rate of two million every second! No wonder researchers call this the "exuberant period" of neural development!

you a glimpse of what's to come, because in the proverbial blink of an eye, you will be taking a picture of him sporting his new superhero backpack as he heads off for his first day of elementary school.

But first a bit about what is going on inside that head of his.

A Short Introduction to Toddler and Preschool Boy Brain Development

When your son was born, most of the neurons in his brain were right where they were supposed to be, and those that hadn't found their rightful place spent the early part of last year migrating there. But these neurons didn't yet know how to talk to each other.

During the first few years of his life, your boy will work overtime to produce connections (synapses) between his neurons. By two years of age, he will have over a hundred trillion synapses, far more than he'll ever need. Nature vigorously prunes or cuts back the synapses your son won't be using by elementary school. You don't have to worry, because this is a natural process. Any one neuron may make fifteen thousand connections. Some of these are trial balloons and as your boy gets better at a particular skill, he won't require all fifteen thousand to complete a task or solve a problem. His brain is set up to leave only those connections that are really necessary for him to respond efficiently. Without this pruning, your boy wouldn't be able to walk or talk properly. In the end, it'll be a leaner, meaner, more efficiently functioning brain for your guy.

Creating Connections

It's a tough world out there for synapse survival. In a classic example of "use it or lose it," some of your son's neural connections will be pruned away due to lack of use. Without a job description and a purpose, a synapse will wither away. The process of creating a surplus of connections is biological; but as parents you can weigh in to a certain degree on what input those neurons will get, which of the paths will be stimulated, and which will be ignored. By providing your son with a variety of experiences—motor, sensory, and cognitive—you'll be giving more of his synapses a workout and a chance to survive the pruning shears.

Your son's genetic blueprint is responsible for the basic wiring plan in his brain and the order in which he will mature. The environment you provide him is there every step of the way interacting with that blueprint. Experience is responsible for fine-tuning those genetically determined connections, helping your son adapt to his particular environment such as where you live, your family configuration, or your cultural identity. *Neural plasticity* is the term neuroscientists use to describe how your boy's brain organization is modified by experience.

We know you are bombarded with information about how to maximize the environment's effect on your boy's wiring, especially from those ads guaranteeing a smarter boy, if only you would use their tapes or books or early learning curriculum. In reality, there is no special program you can buy that will enhance what loving, responsive parenting will provide your son. You and your home are the ideal environment for his boy genes. Give your son ample opportunities to explore his world, keep him safe, and provide the security of your loving support. Have him listen to you sing and talk, send him outside to feel the wind and sun on his face, let him discover the bugs that live in his backyard, and he will have all the natural stimulation his brain needs.

Left Brain, Right Brain

For the first few years of your boy's life, the two hemispheres of his brain will develop at different rates. Your toddler's energy will be focused on growing that left hemisphere, the seat of language, logic, and mathematical skills. As his brain develops, your son will be taking on increasingly complex behaviors and will demonstrate leaps in his cognitive skills.

By elementary school your boy's right hemisphere steps up to the developmental plate. Even though this doesn't happen until his seventh birthday, his right hemisphere isn't being ignored. New connections are developing in your son's corpus callosum, the highway linking the two sides of his brain. Some studies show that the shape, density, and size of your boy's corpus callosum will be smaller on average than that of his female counterpart. Researchers believe this difference makes it more difficult for your guy to do as much multitasking as many girls do and explains some of a boy's delayed

● BABY BOY BRAIN FACT ●
Fuel for Growth

This brainwork your baby boy is doing behind the scenes takes a lot of fuel, so during the first four years of your guy's life he'll be using two times more glucose, the body's primary source of fuel, in his cerebral cortex than you do. Don't worry, you don't have to run out to the pharmacy and buy a glucose supplement. Your boy will get all he needs from digesting the sugar and starch in your breast milk or his formula and the foods you are introducing to him.

mastery of skills as compared to a similarly aged girl. Later on in this chapter we'll talk more about how this difference affects both his behavior and his development.

The Role of Myelin

Synapse creation isn't the only process happening inside your son's brain right now. Your guy may have come equipped with the necessary brain cells, but there was very little myelin, a thick substance coating the length of his brain cells. Think insulation on an electrical cord.

Myelin helps your son's brain deliver messages from one cell to another more efficiently. With limited myelin, it takes a little guy longer to do things than it does an older one. This is why your boy takes a few moments to react when you request that he stop pouring the juice out of his tippy cup. The message needs to be heard, interpreted, and then responded to. That's a lot of information being fired and those connections don't react instantaneously yet. It takes a long time for the myelination process to reach completion. It starts now and will continue even as you watch him receive his

Baby Boy Story

Glenn and Lynn are so proud of twenty-three-month-old Charlie's exploding repertoire of skills. Every night Charlie gives a special running synopsis of his day as they tuck him into his big boy bed and he says his good nights. He starts, "Good night Mama. Good night Papa." He then proceeds with the daily summary. "Good night wagon. Good night doggie. Good night lollipop. Good night truck. Good night big car. Good night 'owie.' Good night peanut butter."

college diploma, although the girls he graduates with may already have finished the process.

The most rapid period of myelination occurs during the first two years of your son's life. The high percentage of fat in myelin (80 percent) is just one reason that fat intake should not be restricted in your boy's diet during those first two years. Pediatricians recommend a diet that contains 50 percent of its calories from fat. Whole milk products are an excellent source of fat for him. After age two, however, fat intake should be limited to about 25–30 percent of calories.

Moving Mountains:
More About Your Little Man in Motion

From that first time your son propelled himself precariously close to the edge of the bed as he rolled over, lunged on all fours for his push car, or toddled on unsteady feet toward his dog, he has been working on exploring the world around him. There will be days when your boy will be inexplicably fussy. A day or two later he'll start walking, or running, or he'll take on the stairs. All that fussiness may be preparation for his next bit of motor mastery. Your boy's world is expanding.

His Gross Motor Skills

On average, at around age two, some little guys may reach 50 percent of adult height. He will achieve this growth marker later than the average twenty months for a girl. He'll also reach puberty later and stop growing later. In the end, though, your boy and his buddies will probably be much stronger and bigger than those same girls.

Baby Boy Story

Jenna called her sister in tears as she drove home from Tommy's preschool parent-teacher conference. His preschool teacher was frustrated and had invited the school director in for the meeting. She told Jenna she couldn't get Tommy to sit still. He had to be doing something with his hands all the time. During circle time, he either had his hands down his pants or would spin himself in circles on the floor, rocking back and forth, until he bumped into whomever was sitting next to him. He seemed to be spending more and more of his day on the time-out bench outside the director's office.

It may take your son longer to grow his boy body, but spend any time on a playground or in a preschool classroom observing toddlers and preschoolers at play and you'll see that he is using his body more than the girls around him. One study of preschool play showed that 63 percent of the boys versus 12 percent of the girls were rated by researchers as being active or extremely active.

A World of Rough-and-Tumble

You can expect your toddler boy to be a study in motion. Far more boys engage in rough-and-tumble play than girls. Your guy will take up more space in his play than your niece does, and he will spend more time pushing the physical limits both of his own body and of the toys that end up broken on your playroom floor. Give a toddler girl a block tower standing between her and what she wants and she will walk around it. If she can't do that, she may cry out to get the attention of the nearest available bystander. Can we say the same for a toddler boy? When presented with the tower obstacle, he will likely knock it down in order to proceed, letting nothing stand between him and the object of his desire.

Motor development follows a specific course in toddlers and preschoolers and it differs for boys and girls. These differences result from the hardwired sequencing pattern their brains follow. Once again the age-old adage that most girls mature earlier than boys holds true. The neural systems that underlie motor development reach full maturity one year later for boys than for girls.

Time to maturity of the brain's motor control systems isn't the only difference between boys' and girls' roads to motor mastery. Researchers using fMRIs are looking at boys' and girls' developing brains as they perform the same task—say, throwing a ball. They are finding that boys and girls use different parts of the brain when they perform identical tasks.

Baby Boy Story

Tiffany took her five-year-old son, Carlos, on a walk in the woods near their home. A tree had fallen over a little creek and Carlos begged his mother for permission to try to go across it. Tiffany was a protective mom but knew she had to give Carlos the freedom to explore, so she reluctantly said yes.

Carlos slowly made his way across the log and returned to her a bit quicker. He repeated the crossing again and again, picking up speed with each subsequent trip. After multiple attempts, Carlos was able to run across the log. That night he told his mom that day had been the best day of his life, assuring her it was even better than his birthday.

Your boy is built to be active. He is going to test the limits of his physical strength. He's going to practice as his brain matures and he'll keep practicing until he gets it right.

Your boy might be a true action figure, moving more than you or his nursery school teacher might prefer. But when he's done playing, he's done. As quickly as he jumps into action, he'll decelerate. His male brain is set to regroup following these energy spurts by going into what neurologists call a rest state.

What to Do with All That Baby Boy Energy?

Here's what you can do to help direct your boy's energy:

- **Go to the playground.** It's filled with larger-than-life toys that beckon a boy's natural exuberance, challenge his skills, and call out to his sense of adventure and danger.
- **Have a ball.** Rolling, kicking, or throwing, it will help his sense of balance and coordination.

Baby Boy Story

Erin planned four-year-old Jason's birthday party just as she had planned his older sister Rachel's. Because they were both Montessori preschoolers, she expected the same level of cooperation and attention from him and the five friends he had invited to their house. Much to Erin's chagrin, however, the boys ran through the scheduled activities in record time and spent the rest of the party wrestling like lion cubs on the living room floor as Erin and her husband, Jeremy, attempted to keep the boys from inflicting bodily harm on each other. Exhausted after the last parents had come to collect their sons, Erin and Jeremy quickly agreed that all Jason's future birthday parties would be at the local gym.

- **Pile on the pillows.** Let him jump from the couch onto a safe surface. He'll want to jump anyway, and you might as well give him a soft landing site.
- **Play blanket tug-of-war.** He'll love the competition and you can cuddle up afterward.
- **Do the hokey pokey!**

Mothers of sons know that all this exploration and rough play come at a certain cost. Your boy will likely be covered with bruises as he jumps, leaps, and bangs his way through his early years. This type of play helps develop the frontal lobe of his brain, the area responsible for regulating behavior. His play is also believed to help the growth and development of synapses and increases the speed at which messages are sent between your son's brain and the rest of his nervous system. This is important for getting your guy ready for

Baby Boy Story

Breda was nervous about enrolling twenty-six-month-old Ari in preschool. When Breda returned to work after her maternity leave, Ari had stayed home with his grandmother. His energy and mobility were increasing just as Grandma's were decreasing. The time had come to enroll him in a preschool program, and Breda was pleased to find that he was thriving. He now had a first friend named Carter.

Every day, the two boys were ecstatic when they first arrived at school, and they would run enthusiastically toward each other. To their parents' amazement, the boys would head bonk, collapse on the floor laughing, and then jump up and start playing. It was a ritual they repeated every morning.

kindergarten. Sitting patiently and waiting his turn, however, will not yet be in your son's repertoire.

Your boy's beautiful head often takes the brunt of these blows, but luckily his larger male cranium is filled with more cerebrospinal fluid than that of a girl. This extra fluid may cushion his brain for the bangs and bumps along his road to motor mastery.

Fine Motor Skills

Your son probably won't need much encouragement to climb the big hill in your backyard, but he may need your support and "Good job!" when it comes to learning how to tie his shoes. In addition to growing his big muscles and learning how to manage them, your boy will be learning how to dress himself and perform other fine motor tasks. He'll be developing those fine motor skills: the tricky task of using his hands to effectively manipulate small objects. Those buttons and zippers may not be easy for your guy. Neither may coloring and holding a pencil. So don't be in a hurry should he decide to take on one of these fine motor challenges. His toddler "Me do!" mentality may take over and you'll have a battle on your hands if you try to button his jacket for him!

There are ways to promote your son's fine motor development and continue to encourage his natural inclinations. Build fine motor practice into everyday activities:

- **Frost cookies.** His creations may not be ready for the food channel but he'll love eating the end result.
- **Build towers.** While you're in the kitchen give him cereal boxes and let him stack them up. He can do the same with canned goods but make sure no one's in the way when he tests the laws of physics by seeing how tall the tower can get.

- **Open lids.** Enclose toys or snacks inside snap-top containers and let him take off the lid to get to the treat.
- **Eat your art.** Finger painting with pudding on wax paper is another fun way to get to your little man through his tummy.
- **More food motivation.** Let your son pull the grapes off their stems, and give him a butter knife to cut up the bananas for your fruit salad. Or let him put the peanut butter on his PB&J.

Your Baby Boy's Cognitive Development

How your son sees and perceives the world through all of his senses shapes how he will remember it. Your little guy will use all his senses to interact with the world around him. He will be thinking, interpreting, understanding, and forming memories of each of these experiences. Researchers call this cognitive development. These skills include

● BABY BOY BRAIN FACT ●
The Differences in Developing Cognitive Skills

Just as there is great overlap between how and when boys and girls develop cognitive skills, there is much variation within the two genders themselves. When we begin to test children for their intellectual mastery we find more boys at the top and the bottom of the scale. More boys than girls are diagnosed with learning disabilities such as dyslexia, delayed speech, and attention-deficit/hyperactivity disorder (ADHD) and more boys are found in classes for gifted and talented children.

information processing, language development, and memory. Your boy is beginning to recall past events, imitate, imagine, and pretend.

A Word or Two About Attention-Deficit Disorder

There's a difference between a boy who is exploring the world using his boy brain and a boy who has a diagnosed disability. Your son is a study in motion and he doesn't always stay focused. At times his impulsive behavior can get him in trouble as he takes things apart in order to understand how they work. Perhaps a family member has made a comment or your day-care provider expressed her concern that your son is "hyperactive." Perhaps no one has said anything, but you are worried. Is your boy just being a boy or is there something wrong?

Boy behavior varies, just as it does for all of us, from serene to frenetic. At the extreme end of the spectrum, some children are

---

 Baby Boy Story

Jana called her mother the evening after Thanksgiving. She had had it with her in-laws' treatment of her four-year-old son, Hap. "I told them I wasn't going to be putting him through this anymore!" Her sister-in-law had complained for the second time in two days that she was worried about her daughter's safety when her cousin Hap was around. Hap's behavior, which had never been a concern for Jana, again became the focus of the dinner table discussion. Hap wouldn't sit still. He played with his food. He touched whomever was sitting next to him. Jana's sister-in-law urged her to take him to a psychiatrist for evaluation. "I stood up for him. I told them he was just a normal little boy. I was so angry at them!" she told her mother. She knew there was nothing wrong with Hap. All the same, she called her mother for reassurance.

---

diagnosed with attention-deficit/hyperactivity disorder (ADHD). The number of children diagnosed with ADHD has increased dramatically over the past twenty years. In a ten-year period, prescriptions for ADHD medicines in American HMOs increased 600 percent. Attention-deficit disorder with hyperactivity is the most commonly diagnosed mental health disorder for children, and boys are three times more likely to be diagnosed with ADHD than girls.

Preschools and day-care centers do not always take into consideration normal boy energy. The only way to tell the difference between normal boy behavior and hyperactivity is with a thorough diagnostic assessment. If you are worried about your son, get an evaluation from a trained professional. Start with your pediatrician, but that may not be the last word. Ask for a referral to someone who specializes in working with hyperactivity disorders. Most experts agree that there are ways to diagnose ADHD accurately, but they are also quick to point out that it may just be a matter of time before a boy grows up, matures, and calms down.

Focusing Behavior

All boys, no matter where they fall on the intellectual or behavioral spectrum, need help focusing and organizing their behavior. You can help your son by giving him

- Simple rules
- A reliable and consistent schedule
- Time outdoors, away from the world of electronic games and TV
- Ample "heads up" time when a transition is about to happen
- An organized room with designated places for his toys, clothes, and day-care supplies
- Your support when he gets it right

Vision

Your boy is a visual kind of guy. He may be more adept at detecting slight movements in his direct field of vision than your niece. He may beat most girls in a picture concentration memory game competition. If asked to remember where an object is, he may excel. Boys outperform girls when it comes to remembering things that involve pictorial stimuli. If you use words to describe a location, a girl tends to remember that information and outperform a boy. But your son will be able to find that red Hot Wheels car in his playroom amidst all the other toys when you have no idea which red Hot Wheels car he is talking about or where to begin looking for it. Fast-forward a few years, however, and he won't see the mayonnaise jar sitting on the refrigerator shelf directly in front of him!

Toddler boys are interested in the contents of your kitchen cabinets. Your boy's brain is skilled at creating systems to organize his world. To understand the cabinets and their contents, he may not

● **BABY BOY BRAIN FACT** ●

Spatial-Visual Discrimination

Researchers looked at the electroencephalograms (EEGs) of five hundred boys and girls starting at two months of age. The researchers found that between birth and the age of six years, boys' and girls' brain development followed different trajectories. Boys' peak activity was found in the areas of the brain associated with spatial-visual discrimination, planning related to gross motor activity, and visual targeting (aiming at an object and trying to hit it with another object).

only remove everything but also try to put it all back again. This same curiosity may drive him in the future to take apart electrical appliances, toys, and the old VCR that doesn't work anymore.

Touch

One way your son may explore his world is by manipulating whatever he can with his hands. He is driven and determined, traits you might sometimes describe as stubborn and obstinate. Not as adept at taking in the big picture, your guy may overestimate his physical skill as he underestimates the fragility of the object in front of him. The frontal lobes of his brain, slower to develop, aren't sending him messages regarding danger and the need for self-control.

Experienced parents can tell how old their new neighbor's son is by how high up fragile household treasures are stowed. Still on the coffee table? The baby isn't pulling himself up yet. Stored on the mantle? He's charging around the house with typical toddler abandon.

Spatial Reasoning

Although your baby boy can't hear as well as a girl his own age, he will, in all likelihood by age three, be better at aiming and hitting both moving and stationary targets. Your boy may not hear you yelling, "Stop!" as he tries to move both himself and whatever object is at hand through space, but he'll surely find his target! And there is research from Johns Hopkins University School of Medicine that suggests that his male brain is better designed for this task.

Your son will also be better at thinking about an object in three dimensions, and he'll have the capacity to rotate that object mentally in a way that his female age mates may not. Your boy understands what an object will look like from a variety of angles without having to move it around in order to figure it out. He may be quicker at navigating a maze or an obstacle course than the average girl. When things all look alike, a girl may not be able to find the landmarks she needs to reach her destination. Your boy may use his sense of direction and distance.

● BABY BOY BRAIN FACT ●
Anatomical Differences

In a study of brain anatomy, researchers found that the inferior parietal lobe, the area of the brain responsible for spatial and mathematical reasoning, is larger in the male brain.

Superior spatial perception is one of the most documented cognitive differences between boys and girls. This difference only increases the older your boy gets. The advantage, which has been documented in boys as young as four-and-a-half, will be reflected down the road when your boy may be more likely to find certain math and science concepts easier to grasp than many of his female classmates. These skills may help your boy figure out maps and understand the directions for building a model. This isn't to say that your son is destined to be a nuclear physicist with only male colleagues. But it does explain in part why males are far more represented in careers that require spatial skills.

Language

Your son's brain structure shapes what interests him in his world. Remember how your son was intrigued by the moving mobile above his bed while many of the girls in the nursery preferred looking at faces? Some of this fascination results from structural differences in the male brain. Believe it or not, the testosterone your son was exposed to *in utero* might take some credit for these differences. It appears those fetal hits of testosterone might continue to impact how your son interacts with his environment. According to some studies, the more testosterone a child is exposed to *in utero,* the less willing he will be to make eye contact with you when he's a toddler, and the fewer words he'll have in his vocabulary at two years of age.

Between birth and the age of five, your son will develop language at a rapid pace, regardless of the amount of testosterone he was exposed to. There is tremendous variability in when toddlers reach language milestones. Language can develop continuously or it can arrive in large bursts following what seems like interminable plateaus. Like all children, your little guy will understand what you're saying to him well before he will be able to "use his words" to tell you what he wants for breakfast. This is called receptive language. Your son's first attempts at expressive language will in all likelihood be a series of nonsensical sounds that imitate the rhythm of your adult speech. But by the age of three, your boy and his buddies will be able to communicate with relative ease, although they may use fewer words than the girls in their preschool class.

In general, most girls develop their verbal skills at a faster rate than the average boy. Because girls talk earlier, they'll start their verbal practicing earlier. By the age of twenty months, girls may have two to three times more words in their vocabularies than boys. Your boy will eventually catch up with the girls. They'll both know about fourteen thousand words by the time they start first grade. Your son may match her numbers of available words, but he may not use them with the same frequency nor utter them just as fast. He may get 125 words out a minute to her average of 250!

You can help your boy's developing language in the following ways:

- **Don't interrupt or finish his sentences for him.** Your boy might be struggling and you want to help, but let him finish his own sentences.
- **Use props—books, puppets, pictures.** Have your son help you tell a story and use his toys as a springboard for your imaginations.
- **Make sure you have his attention before you start talking.** If your boy isn't paying attention to you, stop and wait. He'll get the most out of what you're saying if he is engaged before you start talking.
- **Give him extra one-on-one time.** Your son, more than many girls in his age group, may need some extra practice time to develop his language skills.
- **Sing together.** Your son has difficulty controlling his voice. He'll need some help modulating it but music is one more way to help him use his words.

Autism—A Few Words for the Concerned Parent

Yes, boys do develop more slowly than girls, but if you are concerned about your son's language skills or any other aspect of his development, don't let "he's a boy and boys are slower" deter you from seeking professional consultation. It's no secret that autism affects boys more often than girls. Eighty percent of children diagnosed with autistic disorders are boys.

Autism and other "pervasive developmental disorders" are medical conditions that are not caused by poor parenting. Although researchers are still looking for the causes of autism, there is grow-

Baby Boy Story

Joan is worried about Sam. At twenty-two months, he has stopped using his words. He used to say he loved his mom before he went to sleep, but no longer. Sometimes he'll repeat her sentences verbatim. If she says, "Say thank you, Sam," he'll echo, "Say thank you, Sam." By this age, Sam's older sisters were chattering away. Sam started walking later than his sisters. Otherwise, he is a relatively happy boy. Sam's day-care provider thinks he's just shy, noting he'd rather play with the toys than the other boys at the center. When playing, he lines up his toys in rows, and this worries Joan. Sometimes Sam will answer to his name but not always. He's had a lot of ear infections and was diagnosed with his first one when he was ten days old. Joan has talked to her husband, Mark, about taking Sam to their pediatrician if things don't improve by his second birthday.

ing evidence that genetics interacting with the environment *in utero* cause parts of the brain to develop differently in autistic children. Autism is not a form of mental retardation, but a difference in the way a child's social behavior, communication abilities, and internal interests develop. Some research is focusing on the role of intra-uterine testosterone exposure. Children exposed to higher levels of testosterone *in utero* do have more difficulty making eye contact and developing friendships, and researchers are investigating whether very high levels of testosterone may contribute to the development of autism.

It's not unusual for parents to worry. It's important to remember that each child achieves his developmental milestones at his own pace. Pediatricians do, however, suggest you consult with a professional if your son is

- Not smiling at six months of age
- Not babbling, gesturing, or pointing by twelve months
- Not using single words by sixteen months of age and two word sentences by two years
- Experiencing a loss in language or social skills

You are your son's advocate. Whenever you go to your pediatrician, come prepared. Have specific examples to discuss. It's OK to ask questions and to be persistent. If your physician uses terms you don't understand, ask for explanations. If you are feeling that your concerns have not been addressed or that you need more information, ask for a referral to a specialist such as a developmental pediatrician, psychologist, or a child psychiatrist. Remember, your pediatrician typically has about fifteen minutes to observe your son, but you have a wealth of data. Trust yourself.

Baby Boy Story

Val's daughter, Jenna, invited her entire preschool class to her fourth birthday party. Because Jenna's birthday was in July, Val held the party in their backyard and set up the picnic table under the large willow tree. Val prepared cupcakes for the guests to decorate with frosting and red, white, and blue sprinkles. The girls dutifully sat down on the benches and carefully began decorating. The three boys grabbed their cupcakes, climbed the tree and threw pieces at the girls below.

Your Boy as a Social Being

Now that your son is moving and talking, he may boldly and exuberantly interact with the world around him. During the next few years, you'll observe a leap in your son's social interactions with friends, both real and imaginary. He'll live in a play world of superheroes, bad guys, and action figures. His specialized spatial mechanical skills will shape his play. He'll want to move objects—balls, airplanes, or his own arms and legs—through space.

Early Discipline

As your son becomes more independent, he'll want to exercise more and more control over his environment. If he can jump from the fourth step of the front stoop and land safely, he'll try to jump from the fifth and then the sixth. He's exhilarated by danger. As the parent of a toddler boy, you'll be asked to expand your discipline repertoire.

There are many reasons why you'll find it hard to discipline your son during the next few years. He's curious. He's on the move. His verbal skills are limited. He's trying to make himself understood and it's a frustrating experience for both of you when he can't. His neural response time is slow. He's more capable of getting into mischief, climbing onto countertops and out of his big boy bed. Explaining that he can't do something may not stop your son. Sometimes, you cannot reason with a toddler boy!

Take your boy on a walk when trying to change his behavior. His brain will be engaged while he moves. Don't expect him to look you in the eyes. He is listening, but he may do it better side by side rather than face-to-face.

Tantrums and Frustration

During the next year, your son will probably have his first full-blown temper tantrum. You have done nothing wrong, but the fact is it may take your boy longer to give up his "tantruming" ways than it does for most girls. His circuitry is just overloaded. He's trying to do too much, say too much, and master too much, and when he can't achieve his desired outcome, he'll get frustrated. This is normal. Once the tantrum is in motion, keep your boy safe and be calm. After a tantrum begins, your son physiologically can't stop on demand. His brain is trying to reestablish its equilibrium.

Your son is trying to learn how to solve problems and deal with frustration. When researchers set up an obstacle wall and put a toddler on one side and his or her mother on the other, they were able to observe how boys and girls deal with their frustration. Eventually all the toddlers wanted to get to their mother and they would run into the obstacle. When confronted with this dilemma, boys tried to climb or push the obstacle down. Most girls expressed their frustration by crying, but boys used action in an attempt to solve their problem and your boy may do the same.

Now that your boy is walking and talking, he'll be looking for similar-size people to be with. Your son doesn't quite understand how to be a friend yet. He'll poke, push, bite, and hit your neigh-

---

● BABY BOY BRAIN FACT ●
Boy Bonding

Boys under two usually have less oxytocin, the primary human bonding chemical, than girls.

Baby Boy Story

Susan and Scott were camping with their two children, six-year-old Kaitlin and three-year-old Josh. They loved the Canadian campground because of the beautiful mountain views and the added bonus of a well-equipped playground where the children could frolic to their hearts' content. Kaitlin preferred to sit in the camper, reading. But Josh was at the playground every chance he could get, running around with a new friend. When he asked to go back to the playground after dinner to meet up with his playmate, Susan asked Josh what his new buddy's name was. "Friendy!" he replied gleefully as he set off in the direction of the playground.

bor's son to see how he responds. Your boy may be more impulsive and physical in his play than his older sister ever was.

Your son may not chat empathetically with a friend. Boys often bond with each other by doing things together, not by sitting down and talking. Don't expect your son to come up and talk with you for the sake of conversation. In fact, if a newcomer shows up in his preschool classroom, your son may spend the whole morning playing with him, but not be able to tell you his name.

Toilet Training

Most parents find it difficult to get their sons to stop playing long enough to toilet train them. Although it actually is a brief period in a parent's life, toilet training may seem to stretch on forever and, in fact, boys are slower to train than girls. People will be full of advice as to how to approach this developmental milestone. Do I teach him to sit for both urination and bowel movements? Do I teach him to stand and sit? A potty chair? A toilet potty seat? Which one for which?

If your son is in a day-care home or nursery school, talk to your child-care provider about what the other boys are doing. It can be confusing for your guy if you're not in sync with his child-care provider's equipment. There are many books or articles on the Internet to help you navigate this significant milestone.

Baby Boy Story

Sandy, a thirty-four-year-old yoga instructor, and Jeffrey were visiting friends for the weekend. Nick, their hosts' two-and-a-half-year-old son, was very pleased with the fact that he was potty trained. During dinner he dragged his potty chair into the dining room, proudly pulled off his training pants, and proceeded to pee on the dining room carpet.

Gender Stabilization

By the age of two-and-a-half, your son will develop a curiosity about and an awareness of gender differences. He'll want to imitate his father or older brothers. During his toddler-preschool years, he may develop a clear-cut sense of the fact he is a boy. He'll be conscious that boys have penises and girls don't. He may still think it's possible that his penis might fall off and his sex might change someday. The tantrum he has when you are dressing him in his older sister's hand-me-down pink sweatshirt may be the result of his fear that he'll become a girl!

During this time your son may engage in what you might consider "extreme stereotypical" behavior as he formulates his defini-

Baby Boy Story

Upon her retirement after thirty years of teaching in a Montessori preschool, Annette, a mother of three boys, was asked what surprised her most about teaching children. She answered without hesitation that, try as she might, she couldn't change the fact that the boys wanted to play with guns and the girls did not. Even though there was a zero tolerance policy for bringing toy guns and other play weapons to school, over the years the boys had been extremely creative in creating substitutes. Blocks, twigs, puzzle pieces, and carrot sticks all fulfilled the role.

tion of himself as a man-to-be. Many parents try to raise their boys without stereotypes. They buy pastel-colored clothes and have toy kitchens and dolls in their son's playrooms. Despite these efforts, dolls are often beheaded in an attempt to convert them into guns.

You won't be able to discourage most boys' desire to play with projectiles and weapons. They're having fun! This period, which child psychologists call "gender stabilization," may last through his preschool years. By the age of five, your boy will realize he won't become a girl after all. Then there might be a chance he'll wear that pastel yellow shirt you bought for him.

Friendship and Play

No matter how antisocial your son appears, friendships are very real to him. Your boy will gravitate toward other boys. Gender segregation is found in every preschool. Most girls want to play with girls, and most boys want to play with boys.

The rules are different for boy and girl play. Competition, conflict, and dominance may describe your son's future play life, and girls often respond negatively to these, preferring cooperation for their girl play. Your boy may want to build a taller tower and run faster than his best buddy.

Hardwired to perceive the world with superior spatial mechanical skills, boys' play often takes space. Across the globe, boys wrestle more, fight more, and play games of dominance more than their female age mates. You can look forward to your son and his friends literally bouncing off the walls as they explore friendships and the space around them.

Gender Stereotypes or Normal Boy Behavior?

When asked what determines a boy or girl's toy choice, many people would answer "society's stereotypes." But monkeys are challenging that notion. It turns out monkeys' toy preferences are consistent with human gender choices. Though the monkeys have no concept of a "boy toy" or a "girl toy," male monkeys spend more time playing with cars and balls than female monkeys. The female monkeys spend more time playing with dolls than male monkeys. Presumably, monkey fathers did not object to their sons playing with dolls!

Clearly, there's more at work here than societal expectations. The ball and the car can be propelled through space. They give male monkeys and human boys greater opportunities for rough and active play.

We may not teach our boys to play aggressively. In fact, as parents of a boy, you'll spend a tremendous amount of time trying to *unteach* that type of behavior. As a parent who is continually setting limits on your boy's behavior, you are probably wondering, why are boys more aggressive than girls? Why do they play games of war and destruction? Researchers think that boys are predisposed to higher activity levels in general because of those prenatal testosterone hits.

Don't worry if your boy is being more physical with his buddies than you feel comfortable with. Fighting and verbal aggression are normal for him. He's not being violent; he's just playing. Of course, that doesn't mean you should let him get away with hitting or hurting his playmates. That's where the discipline comes in!

Often parents try to have their son include other boys in their playgroup. Boy play may not include liking a newcomer; it may be about seeing what toys he has and whether he'll be useful in helping build a higher tower.

Developing Social Skills

You can help your boy fine-tune those social skills:

- **Have two of everything.** At first your toddler boy won't be playing with the boys in your playgroup. He'll be playing next to them in what child development specialists call "parallel play." You can decrease the likelihood of bonks and tears by making sure there are plenty of toys (and similar ones) to go around.

- **Keep an eye on the clock.** Timing is everything with two-year-old boys. If your son missed a nap you might consider canceling the play date. None of us are at our best when exhausted.

- **Keep it active.** The more space your boy and his friends have to play the better. Give them the outdoors to explore and they'll be grateful.

Child Care, Preschool, and Beyond

Perhaps you'll be returning to work in the next few months. Perhaps you want your boy to have more opportunities to socialize with other children his own age. Perhaps your son's first academic experience will be in kindergarten. In any case, your son will, within the next few years, find himself in a school-like setting. As the parent of a son, you'll need to be an advocate for him and the male brain that will accompany him to school.

● **BABY BOY BRAIN FACT** ●
Movement in the Classroom

A recent report on preschool education found that the majority of nursery and preschools are stifling the ability of small boys to learn by forcing them to stay indoors and sit still for too long in class.

Accommodating Boy Style

Your boy learns best in motion and some teachers fail to interest this male learning style. Boys often don't want to sit down. Take a boy outside and he'll learn about colors and shapes as he kicks rocks and picks up leaves. The location of a lesson is not as important to a girl. Girls will chatter to themselves wherever they are, talking their way through a lesson. Boys are often silent when working on a project.

Boys get into trouble more in school settings than girls do. Those who think boys are purposefully trying to antagonize teachers have it wrong. They are just trying to stay engaged as best they can. Most boys thrive in competitive academics, not just competitive sports. If the school or day care your son is in is not working well for him, talk with the teacher. Try to figure out a plan that will provide the physical outlets he needs and yet set clear limits for your boy without humiliating him.

When finding a child-care setting or preschool for your boy, make sure there are opportunities for

- **Play.** Play is work for a toddler. Your boy won't be sitting still but, all the same, he'll be learning the skills necessary for elementary school and beyond.
- **Hands-on learning.** Boys learn best in a classroom by touching, moving, climbing on, and building things. They solve problems physically. A lesson on volcanoes comes to life and is far more effective when a boy can add food coloring and vinegar to the baking soda in his volcano and watch it erupt, rather than looking at pictures of Mount St. Helens.
- **Boy topics.** Boys learn best when their thoughts and fantasies can be expressed in their stories and play. The often violent themes that interest boys are uncomfortable for girls and the (typically) female teacher. Your boy will be interested in story time if the books are about his interests and passions.

Baby Boy Story

Rosie couldn't wait for Chris to come home from work. She had taken time off from her work as a math specialist to raise their son, Brian, who was now four years old. Brian was all boy. He gravitated to the dried leaves, dirt, and twig piles whenever he was outside. That day Rosie had taken him to the new public playground. He spent a few minutes on the new equipment and then found the twig and dirt pile off to the side. Brian was busy breaking twigs and talking to himself when he excitedly ran up to his mom. He cried out, "Mom, I figured out stick math. When you break a twig in half it makes two. When you break two twigs, it makes four, and when you break four twigs it makes eight!"

Variety Among Boys

Just as there is variation between the genders, there is tremendous variation within gender. There are many different kinds of boys. They range from the highly physical and competitive to the quiet artist who is just as happy completing his art project as he is wrestling with the boys outdoors during recess. Not all boys turn twigs into guns. Because boys are spread out across the behavioral spectrum, it's difficult to find the "average" boy. Parenting your boy will be an adventure in getting to know who he is.

Leanne, the mother of three-year-old twin boys, will attest to that. This past Halloween she wanted to dress her boys in similar costumes. The boys weren't interested in her plan. Zeb ended up being a ninja warrior and Gabe was a shepherd. It won't be long before your boy will declare himself and let you know what costume he wants for trick-or-treating.

By now, you are firmly established as the parent of a boy. You've likely discovered that mothers and fathers parent differently, based on their own gendered brains. One thing is for sure. You both love your boy without reservation. You both would readily risk danger to protect him. In the next chapter we'll talk about the biological differences in mommy and daddy brains and how it affects the way you both parent. We'll look at resources available to support both of you, and offer some final tips as you forge forward in your on-the-job training of raising a son.

A Baby Boy Is
a Family Affair!
Circles of Support

Larry is a psychiatrist and the father of two sons and a daughter. He once confided to a friend, "We don't have children to feel better, we have children to feel more."

Larry was right, but you don't have to travel alone on this exhilarating yet often overwhelming journey of feelings. There is much wisdom out there for the newly born parent. It comes from the scientific community and the research we have reviewed; from educators who have spent tens of thousands of hours observing children and their behavior; from professionals in your community; from your family, spouse or partner, and the parents in your friendship circle.

The advice will vary, because mothers and fathers do parent differently. Just as your son's personality unfolds based on his male gender, the differences in parenting between you and your spouse are also the result of biology interfacing with experience. How we respond as mothers and fathers is linked to our own gendered brains.

Carl Whitaker, a noted family therapist, describes the differing roles of mothers and fathers by using a tire analogy as a metaphor for the family. If one thinks of the children in the family as the spokes on the wheel, the mother with her female brain is primed for attachment and relationship. She functions as the hub of the wheel, keeping the spokes connected at the center. The father, biologically programmed for risk taking and exploration, functions as the rim, experiencing the external world and the bumps in the road along the way. He protects the spokes and hub. Your spoke, your son, needs both a hub and a rim as he travels the road of his life.

Baby Boy Story

Sophie and David were shopping at the grocery store with their three-year-old twin boys, Michael and Richard, when Sophie started to panic. She couldn't see them. They were chasing each other throughout the store and were several aisles away. David dismissed Sophie's concern as that of an overprotective mother. Sophie shot back, "My umbilical cord is only so long!" With a brain wired for attachment, Sophie wanted to pull them closer. With a brain wired for protection and action, David just had to get them back in sight. The testosterone coursing through David's body allowed him to feel comfortable with his boys' exploration of the store, and within two minutes he had found them in the produce section.

The Biology of Mother and Father Brains

While your son began growing his male brain *in utero,* you, his parents, were each growing a mother or father brain. Advances in research not only demonstrate the differences between the male and female brains but also the difference between a maternal and a nonmaternal brain. The dramatic hormonal fluctuations that occur during pregnancy, birth, and lactation are in part responsible for re-modeling the female brain. Pregnancy and motherhood change the structure of the female mammal's brain, making mothers attentive to their young and better equipped to care for them. Brain pathways that handle the stressors of a child-free existence require less efficiency, resiliency, and resourcefulness than the brain of a sleep-deprived mother attempting to juggle work, laundry, a diaper bag, a car seat, and a fussy baby.

Researchers tell us that the brain continues to develop through-out the human life span. New pathways form in response to new challenges and experiences. Before becoming a parent, how many of us have had the experience of calming a screaming baby while driving fifty-five miles an hour and listening to the latest world news crisis, in an attempt to arrive at the sitter's with enough time to get to work by 8:30 AM? A brain researcher describes the drama of becoming a parent as a "revolution for the brain."

A Mother's Response

New research indicates that the fluctuations in hormones during pregnancy permanently alter the neural pathways in a mother's brain.

⁛ Mommy Brain Story

Amy came into her therapist's office in tears. She had been a high-powered manager in a large software company before giving birth to her son, David. She and her husband had decided for the first few years of David's life that she would stay home with him. Now she had become the mommy who forgot things all the time, who got frustrated at little things, and who didn't work in a big office building in the city like Daddy.

She complained her son didn't see her as the woman who had a master's degree and who formerly managed million-dollar accounts. She knew that she had been the smart girl since elementary school, but Amy was afraid her son was coming to the conclusion that Mommy, in fact, might not be too bright.

Her therapist told her not to worry. Amy's brain was fine, just adapting to its new role as a mother of a young child. Her son's perception of her would be fine as well, her therapist added.

Women frequently come into their OB visits asking questions not only about their bodies but also about their brains.

"I'm scattered. I forget things all the time. Will I get my brain back?" The diagnosis is "pregmentia," we joke. But in fact the pregnant woman and her developing mother brain are undergoing some startling changes.

In a Canadian study, researchers took blood samples from thirty-four couples at different times during pregnancy and shortly after birth. They monitored the levels of oxytocin, cortisol, and prolactin in both men and women.

Oxytocin is one of nature's chief tools for creating a mother. The number of oxytocin receptors in the expectant mother's brain multiplies dramatically near the end of her pregnancy. This makes for a more responsive mother. Mothers continue producing oxytocin as a result of breast-feeding and holding their babies. Babies who are responded to are more responsive, and this makes moms respond more readily, thus setting a positive feedback loop in motion. With oxytocin levels elevated, new mothers' brains are producing new synapses, creating the hardwiring necessary for maternal behaviors.

Released in response to signals from the amygdala, cortisol is a stress hormone that is also an important indicator of attachment. Mothers with higher cortisol levels can detect their baby's smell more readily than mother's with lower levels. These mothers also describe feeling a greater closeness with their babies.

Mommy Brain Fact   *Under the Influence*

An interesting side effect of maternal oxytocin surges is that moms not only bond with their babies, but with any male who happens to be around. A good reason for dads to be available during this time!

Prolactin, the hormone responsible for lactation, was the last hormone studied. Babies by their very nature give us the opportunity to have our brain altered. Your son's demands that you hold him and feed him multiple times during the day and night result in higher prolactin levels. And when the brain is exposed to prolactin for long periods of time, the opioid system is stimulated. Family bonding can be a real high for the new mother!

With all these hormonal influences at work, women are primed for the style of nurturance associated with "mothering." The oxytocin that is coursing through her body is likely to heighten her awareness of her baby and his needs. In most cases it's Mom for whom a toddler calls out when he gets his "owie," and most mothers will respond with expressions of direct empathy. New mothers are more likely to relinquish their personal time and need for independence in order to care for their new sons. It is quite common for a mother to struggle with maintaining so-called "selfish" activities, such as personal hygiene and exercise, during the early months of her son's life.

A Father's Response

But Mom is not the only one experiencing hormonal upheaval during pregnancy and the early days of parenting! In the same Canadian research studies that examined mothers' levels of oxytocin, prolactin, and cortisol, researchers suggested that there is much more to masculinity than testosterone. Although testosterone is certainly important in driving men to conceive a child, it takes a collection of other hormones to make a father.

In a study published in the *Mayo Clinic Proceedings,* researchers found that new fathers have higher levels of estrogen, the hormone typically associated with women. During pregnancy and the postpartum period, men go through a hormonal shift just as their partners do. Surprisingly, 90 percent of men report experiencing occasional physical symptoms such as nausea and weight gain during their wife's pregnancy. It turns out that nature may play a role in preparing men as well as women to be committed parents.

These studies also found that fathers' prolactin and cortisol levels were in flux. In the three weeks before a child's birth, fathers' prolactin levels went up approximately 20 percent, and cortisol levels were two times greater during this period than during early pregnancy.

> **Daddy Brain Fact**   *Dads Have Hormones Too!*
> For the first month of a newborn's life, her father's testosterone levels decrease as much as 33 percent. Don't worry, Dads. Testosterone will return to its pre-pregnancy levels. One psychologist suggests that the decline is responsible for helping a father bond with his child and allows for the nurturing aspects of Dad's personality to be present during the first few weeks of his child's life.

Although present and active during bonding in the mother and infant, vasopressin also plays a role in the new father's neural chemistry. Vasopressin, a hormone made in the hypothalamus and stored in the pituitary gland, is known to influence pair bonding. Vasopressin is released in the male in response to nearness and touch. When Daddy is at home during those first few days, vasopressin is released at high levels and helps him bond with his new son.

✴ Daddy Brain Story

Scott was going to stay home alone with the baby for the first time since his birth. Kirsty was going to go to the grocery store for just a few items. She was nervous, as she wasn't supplementing her breast milk with any bottles. She began to provide Scott with a litany of things he could and should do for their son in her absence. Finally, in exasperation, Scott looked at her and exclaimed, "Kirsty, I may not have breasts but I do have a brain!"

Following those first early weeks of parenting, a father's testosterone levels will reassert themselves at previous levels, and his male brain wiring will set the stage for a father's unique style of nurturance.

A boy's father will have a more physical, rough-and-tumble relationship with his son than a boy's mom will. A father's spatial and mechanical skills provide for a different set of opportunities for a son to interact with the world. A father is more likely to engage in lifting his son in the air, hugging him and moving him around carefully but more rapidly than Mom. And as your son gets older, it will in all likelihood be Dad throwing balls, wrestling, and teaching his boy how to throw darts.

A father's interactions will likely come more in short, active bursts rather than the ongoing, hands-on parenting that a mother provides. Dad will get in there and stir things up with father energy just when Mom thinks they have settled their boy down. Dad will set up competitive race courses in the living room, through the hall, and out into the kitchen. He'll encourage a boy to push his physical limits, often to Mom's dismay.

Mom and Dad Under One Roof

As mothers and fathers express their gendered brain through parenting, stylistic differences become inevitable. If conflicts haven't come up yet between you and your spouse, don't be surprised when they do.

Fathers think that mothers worry too much about their children. Mothers, responding to their own biology, often parent with emotional intensity far greater than that of their husbands. As moms and dads play with their son on the backyard swing set, Mom is likely to worry about her boy's safety as Dad pushes the swing higher and higher. As their boy yells out, "Look at me!" moms will likely say something along the lines of, "Be careful. Don't go too high!" But dads may encourage their boy to see just how high he can swing. And then if he happens to fall from the swing, Dad may think that

---

A MOTHER AND FATHER BRAIN STORY

Maggie and Lloyd took their boys, ages two and five, up to the mountain for a cross-country skiing weekend. After skiing with two-year-old Larry on their backs, the parents returned to the lodge and gave their son a chance to run around. Lloyd grabbed a sled and took Larry up a small hill when Maggie yelled after Lloyd about how icy the hill was. Lloyd wasn't worried. Just then Larry came flying off the sled face down. By the time Maggie reached him, he was sitting up with blood dripping from the scrapes on his face. She was furious but Larry was laughing, and Lloyd was ready to take his son up for another run.

Mom is being too soft as she comforts her boy and covers his "boo-boos" with kisses.

Loaded with estrogen and oxytocin, mothers are primed for the intensity that parenting a newborn requires. The majority of mothers win the gold medal when it comes to nurturing behaviors such as feeding, diapering, and caring for an ill child. And when asked, mothers say they like performing these caring duties more than their husbands do.

Just as their sons use fewer words than their female age mates, fathers continue to use fewer words in talking to their boy than Mom will. Fathers want "just the facts, ma'am," and mothers want to talk about how their son feels about the facts. Mom may encourage her son to "use his words" but Dad is more likely to tell his boy to "shake it off." A father may set up a race between his three-year-old daughter and her best boy buddy. If the girl wins and her friend bursts into tears, they'll be no cuddles and words of support for him from the two fathers in the room. The mothers will likely ask him what they could do to make it all better.

Given moms' greater interest and desire to perform the "basics" of early parenting, they tend to perform these tasks more than their husbands. In fact, babies get used to it. The majority of infants and toddlers tend to call out first for Mom's caring touch. Your son not only may be interested in being comforted by Mom for the first few years, he may play more with Mom, who is more attentive to all the nuances of his behavior.

Mothers are more interested in spending longer periods of time with their sons. Utilizing her more acute senses to stay attuned to her baby's needs, mothers are lighter sleepers when they have a baby in the house. A father is less likely to hear his son cry at night and is more likely to be annoyed if he awakens him.

⁑ Mommy Brain Story

From an early age, Susan had always enjoyed being the center of her peers' social scene. Spencer, her five-year-old son, was different. He was just as content being by himself as he was playing with other kids. One weekend, the preschool director's son was having his fifth birthday party and Spencer wasn't invited. It was Susan, not Spencer, who was devastated by the lack of an invitation. Susan made sure to have a very special play date set up for Spencer the afternoon of the party. Whether he was aware the play date was scheduled during the same time as the party or not, Susan felt better making sure he wasn't alone the day of the party.

With greater peripheral vision, mothers literally seem to have eyes in the back of their heads. At any given moment she is conscious of where her son is or what her son needs. Unless specifically asked to keep an eye on his boy, a father may assume his son is fine.

Differences in Discipline

Mothers and fathers differ when it comes to disciplining their sons. Dads are often quick to intervene and set boundaries in a clear manner. Mom often interprets Dad's clarity as brusque and too harsh. Mothers are worried about how their sons feel at the end of the discipline process. For mothers, getting the message across is often secondary to preserving a son's self-esteem. Believing that boys need a father to keep track of them and hold them accountable, fathers feel responsible for making sure the message is primary.

So What Are Two Loving Parents to Do?

- **Accept that you are different** and appreciate that these differences broaden your son's life experience. At times it is important to agree to disagree.
- **Give each other the opportunity to spend time alone with your son.** Your son needs both of you and both of you need time to practice being in charge. It's easy for fathers to turn over the parenting job to Mom if she happens to be around. If a mom isn't present, dads really do know how to take care of their sons.
- **Give yourself time alone without your son.** It's important for a mom to learn how to take care of herself even when she becomes a mother!
- **Remember, before you were parents, you were a couple.** Fathers report feeling neglected by their wives who frequently put the kids ahead of the couple. Take care of your relationship; it will sustain both of you over time.
- **Let dads roughhouse.** Dads know how to play physically with their boys. Your boy loves the stimulation and this type of play will not make him aggressive. Mothers often think Dad is over-stimulating their boy. Dad is in fact teaching his son valuable lessons about self-control!

Where Else Can You Find Support?

You don't have to parent alone. Use your extended family, both biological and otherwise. Your parents, friends, and members of your support network are all there to support you. Ask questions; glean from the wisdom of their experience. You may not always agree with their advice, but an alternative perspective can be valuable.

The Expert Community

Experts can weigh in as well with parenting advice. The Gurian Institute is one of many organizations available in assisting you as a parent. On the Web site you will find recommendations for articles, additional Web sites, and books on brain research that will support you as you begin your parenting adventure. You can find us at www.gurianinstitute.com. The Institute focuses on providing families with a crucial understanding of how boys and girls learn and grow differently.

Your community will have any number of local and national organizations to help provide you with advice. There are literally millions of options. A quick check on the Internet resulted in 2,700,000 options when "parenting advice" was searched! Whom do you listen to? Which option is a good fit for you and your family? After talking to your pediatrician and other sources of support, you and your spouse will in the end need to trust yourselves.

A Special Note for Dads

Your son needs you. Even though the lion's share of early parenting tasks may fall to your wife, especially if she is breast-feeding, you play a significant role.

According to the American Academy of Pediatrics, "When fathers play a visible and nurturing role in their children's lives, the children have better emotional and social outcomes and are more likely to have stronger coping and adaptation skills, be better equipped to solve problems, stay in school longer, have longer-lasting relationships and have a higher work productivity."

A Special Note for Overworked, Exhausted Moms

Give up trying to be the super mom. There are no perfect moms. There are, however, "good enough" moms. Spend some time talking with other mothers and your husband about what you are willing to let go of. The house doesn't have to be perfect and you don't need to be back in your skinny jeans this month. Ask yourself what tasks you can share with your husband. And if he cleans the toilet bowl, can you allow him to do it his way?

A Final Word

Nanette is a talented OB-GYN. She is married to a well-respected internist. The couple had Tanya, now five, while they were in their residency programs. Will, their second child, was born just last year.

One day, standing at the doctors' lab, Nanette confessed to her nurse that if she had done anything else seven days a week, twenty-four hours a day for five years, she would feel as if she had mastered the task. Parenting left her feeling chronically incompetent. Just when she felt like she understood what Tanya or Will needed and that she was on top of her mothering game, one or the other would reach a new developmental milestone, providing her with new issues and challenging her latest approach to parenting.

Nanette is not alone. There will be times when you will feel—just as she does—masterful and ready to give advice to other parents. Other times you will feel woefully inadequate. Just like your son, mothers and fathers go though phases. Give your boy and yourself time. You are all under construction and we can assure you that with love, good humor, and mutual support, you'll all be able to deal with whatever happens next.

Sources

Introduction

Allen, J. S., & others. "Neuroscience for Kids: She Brains–He Brains." Society for Neuroscience. Retrieved from http://faculty .washington.edu/chudler/heshe.html.

Drubach, D. *The Brain Explained.* Upper Saddle River, N.J.: Prentice-Hall, 2000.

Eliot, L. *What's Going On in There? How the Brain and Mind Develop in the First Five Years of Life.* New York: Bantam Books, 1999.

Elium, D., & Elium, J. *Raising a Son.* Berkeley, Calif.: Celestial Arts, 2004.

"Gender and the Brain." *Brain Briefings.* Society for Neuroscience, 1998. Retrieved from www.sfn.org/briefings/gender.brain.html.

"Gender Differences." SlideShare. Retrieved from www.slideshare. net/readysetpresent/gender-differences-powerpoint.

Gurian, M. *The Wonder of Boys.* New York: Tarcher, 1997.

Gurian, M., & Stevens, K. *The Minds of Boys.* San Francisco: Jossey-Bass, 2005.

Laliberte, R. "The Difference Between Boys and Girls." *Parents,* Mar. 2006. Retrieved from www.parents.com/toddlers/ development/behavioral/difference-between-boys-girls/.

LeVay, S. *The Sexual Brain.* Cambridge, Mass.: A Bradford Book, 1993.

Moir, A., & Jessel, D. *Brain Sex: The Real Difference Between Men and Women.* New York: Dell, 1989.

Sax, L. *Why Gender Matters.* New York: Doubleday, 2005.

Springer, S. P., & Deutsch, G. *Left Brain Right Brain* (4th ed.). New York: Freeman, 1993.

Chapter One

Achiron, R., Lipitz, S., & Achiron, A. "Sex-Related Differences in the Development of the Human Fetal Corpus Callosum." *Prenatal Diagnosis,* 2001, *21*(2), 116–120.

Allen, L. S., & Gorski, R. A. "Sexual Dimorphism of the Anterior Commissure and Massa Intermedia of the Human Brain." *Journal of Comparative Neurology,* 1991, *312,* 97–104.

Baron-Cohen, S., Luthmaya, S., & Knikmeyer, R. *Prenatal Testosterone in Mind: Amniotic Fluid Studies.* Cambridge, Mass.: MIT Press, 2004.

Becker, J. B., & others (eds.). *Sex Differences in the Brain: From Genes to Behavior.* New York: Oxford University Press, 2007.

Cahill, L. "His Brain, Her Brain." *Scientific American,* May 2005, pp. 40–47.

Chudler, E. "Neuroscience for Kids." 1996–2008. Retrieved July 23, 2007, from http://faculty.washington.edu/chudler/neurok.html.

de Lacoste, M., Holloway, R., & Woodward, D. "Sex Differences in the Fetal Human Corpus Callosum." *Human Neurobiology,* 1986, 5(2), 93–96.

Goodwin, M. "Can I Choose My Baby's Sex?" *BabyCenter.* n.d. Retrieved from www.babycenter.com/404_can-i-choose-my-babys-sex_1933.bcA.

Graham, J. "Boosting Baby's Brain Before Birth." *Parents.com*. Sept. 2000. Retrieved Aug. 21, 2007, from www.parents.com/parents/story.jsp?storyid=/Templatedata/parents/story/data/1001.xml.

Harvard School of Public Health. "Pregnant Women Carrying Boys Eat More Than Those Carrying Girls." Press Release. June 6, 2003. Retrieved Aug. 8, 2007, from www.hsph.harvard.edu/news/press-releases/archives/2003-releases/press06062003.html.

Healy, J. M. *Your Child's Growing Mind.* New York: Broadway Books, 2004.

Hines, M. *Brain Gender.* New York: Oxford University Press, 2004.

Hopson, J. L. "Fetal Psychology." *Psychology Today,* Sept.-Oct. 1998, *31*(5), 44.

Human Genome Project. "20 Facts About the Human Genome." *Welcome Trust Sanger Institute,* Cambridge, England. Aug. 10, 2007. Retrieved from www.sanger.ac.uk/HGP/draft2000/facts.shtml.

Ingemarsson, I. "Gender Aspects of Preterm Birth." *BJOG: An International Journal of Obstetrics and Gynecology,* 2003, 110.s20, 34–38.

Kimura, D. "Sex Differences in the Brain." SciAm.com. May 13, 2002. Retrieved Aug. 6, 2007, from www.sciam.com/article.cfm?id=00018E9D-879D-1D06-8E49809EC588EEDF&page=1.

Marsas, L. "He Thinks, She Thinks." *Discover.* July 5, 2007. Retrieved July 27, 2007, from http://discovermagazine.com/2007/brain/she-thinks.

Murkoff, H., Eisenberg, A., & Hathaway, S. *What to Expect the First Year.* New York: Workman, 2003.

"Pregnancy." *Medline Plus*. U.S. National Library of Medicine, National Institutes of Health. Jan. 2007. Retrieved Aug. 2007, from www.nlm.nih.gov/medlineplus/pregnancy.html.

Rosen, P. "Boy or Girl: Can You Choose?" *American Baby*. May 2005. Retrieved from www.parents.com/parents/story.jsp?page=2& storyid=/templatedata/ab/story/data/BoyOrGirl06152005.xml.

Shors T. J., & Miesegaes, G. "Testosterone in Utero and at Birth Dictates How Stressful Experience Will Affect Learning in Adulthood." *Proceedings of the National Academy of Sciences,* Oct. 15, 2002, *99,* 13955–13960.

"Stress in Pregnancy Means Boys Will Be Stronger." News-Medical Net, Jan. 25, 2006. Retrieved Aug. 11, 2007, from www.news -medical.net/?id=15613.

"Testes: Differentiation." *Human Embryology*. Universities of Fribourg, Lausanne and Bern (Switzerland). Retrieved Aug. 13, 2007, from www.embryology.ch/anglais/ugenital/diffmorpho02.html.

UNSW Embryology. January 2007. University of New South Wales, Sydney, Australia. Retrieved Aug. 13, 2007, from http:// embryology.med.unsw.edu.au/embryo.htm.

Villar, J., & others. "World Health Organization Randomized Trial of Calcium Supplementation Among Low Calcium Intake Pregnant Women." *American Journal of Obstetrics and Gynecology,* 2006, *194*(3), 639–649.

Zeisel, S. "The Fetal Origins of Memory: The Role of Dietary Choline in Optimal Brain Development." *Journal of Pediatrics.* 2006, *149*(5), S131–S136.

Chapter Two

"Babies' Brain Development Immediately After Birth." *Medical News Today,* Dec. 29, 2003. Retrieved from www.medicalnewstoday .com/articles/5059.php.

BabyCenter Medical Advisory Board. "Help Your Child Understand Speech and Concepts." *BabyCenter.* n.d. Retrieved from www .babycenter.com/0_help-your-child-understand-speech-and -concepts_11734.bc.

Baron-Cohen, S. *The Essential Difference.* New York: Basic Books, 2003.

Baron-Cohen, S., Knickmeyer, R. C., & Belmonte, M. K. "Sex Differences in the Brain: Implications for Explaining Autism." *Science,* Nov. 4, 2005, *310*(5749), 819–823.

Caplan, F. *The First Twelve Months of Life.* New York: Bantam Books, 1984.

Cassidy, J., & Ditty, K. "Gender Differences Among Newborns on a Transient Otoacoustic Emissions Test for Hearing." *Journal of Music Therapy,* 2001, *37*, 28–35.

"Cognition Through the Lifespan." Retrieved from www.columbia. edu/itc/hs/nursing/n4225/2004_02/lect05Slides.pdf.

Cone-Wesson, B., & Ramirez, G. "Hearing Sensitivity in Newborns Estimated from ABRs to Bone-Conducted Sounds." *Journal of the American Academy of Audiology,* 1997, *8*, 299–307.

Dalton, J. "Male Circumcision—See the Harm to Get a Balanced Picture." *The Journal of Men's Health and Gender,* 2007, *4*(3), 312–317.

"Development of Cochlear Active Mechanisms in Humans Differs Between Gender." *Neuroscience.* Letters, 1996, *220*, 49–52.

Don, M., Ponton, C., Eggermont, J. J., & Masuda, A. "Gender Differences in Cochlear Response Time: An Explanation for Gender Amplitude Differences in the Unmasked Auditory Brainstem Response." *Journal of the Acoustical Society of America,* 1995, *94*, 2135–2146.

El-Hout, Y., & Khauli, R. "The Case for Routine Circumcision." *Journal of Men's Health and Gender,* 2007, *4*(3), 300–305.

Eliot, L. *What's Going On in There? How the Brain and Mind Develop in the First Five Years of Life.* New York: Bantam Books, 1999.

Frederikse, M., & others. "Sex Differences in the Inferior Parietal Lobe." *Cerebral Cortex,* 1999, *9,* 896–901.

"Gender and Pain." *Brain Briefings.* Society for Neuroscience, May 2007. Retrieved from www.sfn.org/index.cfm?pagename =brainBriefings_gender_ and_pain.

"Gender and the Brain." *Brain Briefings.* Society for Neuroscience, 1998. Retrieved from www.sfn.org/briefings/gender.brain.html.

"Gender Differences." SlideShare. Retrieved from www.slideshare. net/readysetpresent/gender-differences-powerpoint.

Green, A. "Masturbation in Young Children." Drgreene.com, 2007. Retrieved Sept. 14, 2007, from www.drgreene.com/21_606 .html.

Halpern, D. F. *Sex Differences in Cognitive Abilities.* Mahwah, N.J.: Erlbaum, 2000.

Healy, J. M. *Your Child's Growing Mind.* New York: Broadway Books, 2004.

Hill, G. "The Case Against Circumcision." *The Journal of Men's Health and Gender,* 2007, *4*(3), 318–323.

Multnomah County Library. *Brain Development: Birth to Six.* n.d. Retrieved from www.multcolib.org/birthtosix/braindev.html.

NCHS United States Clinical Growth Chart. Retrieved from www.cdc. gov/nchs/about/major/nhanes/growthcharts/clinical_charts.htm.

"Newborn Brains Grow Vision and Movement Regions First." *Science Daily,* Feb. 13, 2007. Retrieved from www.science daily.com/releases/2007/02/070208131703.htm.

Parrish, T. "Boys' Behavior: Why Boys Behave the Way They Do?" *Brainy-Child.com.* Dec. 12, 2007. Retrieved from www .brainy-child.com/article/boys-behavior.shtml.

"Physical Development 2–6." *CliffNotes.com.* Retrieved Dec. 7, 2007, from www.cliffnotes.com/WileyCDA/CLiffsReviewTopic/topic/ARticledld -26831.articleld-26772.html.

Robledo, S. J. "Developmental Milestone: Self-Care." *BabyCenter,* n.d. Retrieved from http://parentcenter.babycenter.com/0 _developmental-milestone-self-care_63974.pc.

Sato, H., & others. "Sexual Dimorphism and Development of the Human Cochlea." *Acta Otolaryngologica,* 1991, *111,* 1037–1040.

Schoen, E. "Circumcision Is a Lifetime Vaccination with Many Benefits." *Journal of Men's Health and Gender,* 2007, 4(3), 306–311.

Sullivan, D. "Your 18-Month-Old's Social and Emotional Development: Making Friends." *BabyCenter,* n.d. Retrieved from www.babycenter.com/0_your-18-month-olds-social-and -emotional-development-making-f_1213792.bc.

Springer, S. P., & Deutsch, G. *Left Brain Right Brain* (4th ed.). New York: Freeman, 1993.

Task Force on Circumcision. "American Academy of Pediatrics: Circumcision Policy Statement." *Pediatrics,* 1999, *103*(3), 686–693.

"Toddler's First Steps: A 'Best Chance' Guide to Parenting Your Six-Month- to Three-Year-Old." Retrieved from www.health.gov. bc.ca/cpa/publications/firststeps.pdf.

Chapter Three

Ames, L. B., & Ilg, F. *Your Three-Year-Old: Friend or Enemy.* New York: Dell, 1985.

Ashley, M., & Lee, J. *Women Teaching Boys.* Trentham Books, London: 2003.

BabyCenter Medical Advisory Board. "The ABCs of Toilet Training." *BabyCenter.* Sept. 2006. Retrieved from www.babycenter. com/0_the-abcs-of-toilet-training_4399.bc.

BabyCenter Medical Advisory Board. "Help Your Child Understand Speech and Concepts." *BabyCenter.* n.d. Retrieved from www .babycenter.com/0_help-your-child-understand-speech-and -concepts_11734.bc.

BabyCenter Medical Advisory Board. "Toilet Training: What Works?" *Baby Center.* n.d. Retrieved from www.babycenter.com/0 _toilet-training-what-works_4397.bc.

Baron-Cohen, S. *The Essential Difference.* New York: Basic Books, 2003.

Baron-Cohen, S., Knickmeyer, R. C., & Belmonte, M. K. "Sex Differences in the Brain: Implications for Explaining Autism." *Science,* Nov. 4, 2005, *310*(5749), 819–823.

Beighle, A., & others. "Children's Physical Activity During Recess and Outside of School." *Journal of School Health,* Dec. 2006, *76*(10), 516–520.

Bland, J. "About Gender: Sex Differences." Retrieved from www .gender.org.uk/about/07neur/77_diffs.htm.

Blanton, R. E., & others. "Gender Differences in the Left Inferior Frontal Gyrus in Normal Children." *NeuroImage,* 2004, *22,* 626–636.

Boyatzis, C., Chazan, E., & Ting, C. Z. "Preschool Children's Decoding of Facial Emotions." *Journal of Genetic Psychology,* 1993, *154,* 375–382.

Boyd, H. "Gender Differences: First Grade." Education.com. www .education.com/magazine/article/Gender_First_Grade/.

Bremner, J. D., & others. "Gender Differences in Cognitive and Neural Correlates in Remembrance of Emotional Words." *Psychopharmacology Bulletin,* 2001, *35,* 55–74.

Caplan, F. *The Second Twelve Months of Life.* New York: Bantam Books, 1984.

De Bellis, M. D., & others. "Sex Differences in Brain Maturation During Childhood and Adolescence." *Cerebral Cortex,* June 2001, *11*(6), 552–557.

de Courten-Myers, G. M. "The Human Cerebral Cortex: Gender Differences in Structure and Function." *Journal of Neuropathology and Experimentalogy Neurology,* 1999, *58*(3), 217–226.

Duff, S. J., & Hampson, E. "A Sex Difference on a Novel Spatial Working Memory Task in Humans." *Brain and Cognition,* 2001, *47*(3), 470–493.

Eals, M., & Silverman, I. "The Hunter-Gatherer Theory of Spatial Sex Differences: Proximate Factors Mediating the Female Advantage in Recall of Object Arrays." *Ethology and Sociobiology,* 1994, *15,* 95–105.

Eliot, L. *What's Going On in There? How the Brain and Mind Develop in the First Five Years of Life.* New York: Bantam Books, 1999.

Fales, E. "A Comparison of the Vigorousness of Play Activities of Preschool Boys and Girls." *Child Development,* June 1937, *8*(2), 144–158.

"Frequently Asked Questions." n.d. Retrieved from www.totsand toddlers.com/faq.

"Gender Differences in Language Appear Biological: Language Processing More Abstract in Girls, More Sensory in Boys." *EurekAlert.* Retrieved from www.eurekalert.org/pub_releases/2008-03/nu-gdi030308.php.

"Gender Differences in the Human Cerebral Cortex: More Neurons in Males; More Processes in Females." *Journal of Child Neurology,* 1999, *14*(2), 98–107.

Gibson, K. R. "Myelinisation and Behavioural Development: A Comparative Perspective on Questions of Neoteny, Altricity and Intelligence." In K. R. Gibson & A. C. Petersen (eds.), *Brain Maturation and Cognitive Development.* New York: Aldine De Gruyter, 1985.

Gur, R. C., & others. "Sex Differences in Brain Gray and White Matter in Healthy Young Adults." *Journal of Neuroscience,* 1999, *19,* 4065–4972.

Gur, R. C., & others. "An fMRI Study of Sex Differences in Regional Activation to a Verbal and Spatial Task." *Brain and Language Journal,* 2000, *74,* 346–350.

Gryn, G., & others. "Brain Activation During Human Navigation: Gender-Different Neural Networks as Substrate of Performance." *Nature Neuroscience,* Apr. 2000, *3*(4), 404–408.

Gurian, M., & others. *Boys & Girls Learn Differently!* San Francisco: Jossey-Bass, 2001.

Haier, R. J., & others. "The Neuroanatomy of General Intelligence: Sex Matters." *Neuroimage,* 2005, *25,* 320–327.

Haines, C. "Sequencing, Co-Ordination and Rhythm Ability in Young Children." *Child Care, Health and Development,* Sept. 2003, *29*(5), 395–409.

Hall, J. A., & Matsumoto, D. "Gender Differences in Judgments of Multiple Emotions from Facial Expressions." *Emotion,* 2004, *4,* 201–206.

Halpern, D. F., & others. "The Science of Sex Differences in Science & Mathematics." *Psychological Science in the Public Interest,* Aug. 2001, *8*(1), 1–51.

Hanlon, H., Thatcher, R., & Cline, M. "Gender Differences in the Development of EEG Coherence in Normal Children." *Developmental Neuropsychology,* 1999, *16*(3), 479–506.

Harmel, K. "Language Delay and Gender." *American Baby,* Apr. 2004. Retrieved from www.parents.com/parents/story.jsp?storyid=/

templatedata/ab/story/data/ABApr2004LanguageDelay
_04212004.xml.

Healy, J. M. *Your Child's Growing Mind.* New York: Broadway Books, 2004.

Hernandez, C. G., & others. *Primary Care Pediatrics.* Philadelphia: Lippincott Williams & Wilkins, 2007, p. 117.

Jarvis, P. "Rough and Tumble Play: Lessons in Life." *Evolutionary Psychology,* 2006, *4,* 330–346.

Johnson, L. A. "Behavior Drug Spending Up: More Kids Taking Pills for ADHD." *Associated Press,* May 17, 2004.

Kansaku, K., & Kitazawa, S. "Imaging Studies on Sex Differences in the Lateralization of Language." *Neuroscience Research,* 2001, *41,* 333–337.

Karges-Bone, L. *More Than Pink and Blue: How Gender Can Shape Your Curriculum.* Carthage, Ill.: Teaching and Learning Company, 1998.

Kimura, D. "Sex Differences in the Brain." *Scientific American,* 1992, *10,* 118–125.

Kimura, D. *Sex and Cognition.* Cambridge, Mass.: MIT Press, h1999.

Kimura, D. "The Hidden Mind." *Cerebral Cortex,* June 2001, *11*(6), 552–557.

Klomsten, A. T., Skaalvik, E. M., & Espnes, G. A. "Physical Self Concept and Sports: Do Gender Differences Still Exist?" *Sex Roles: A Journal of Research.* Retrieved from http://goliath. ecnext.com/coms2/gi_0199-708695/Physical-self-concept-and-sports.html.

Labarthe, J. C. "Are Boys Better Than Girls at Building a Tower or a Bridge at 2 Years of Age?" *Archives of Diseases of Childhood,* 1997, *77,* 140–144.

Larson, J., & Gidley, C. "Effects of Gender and Age on Motor Exam in Typically Developing Children." *Developmental Neuropsychology,* 2007, *32*(1), 543–562.

Lawton, C. A., & Kallai, J. "Gender Differences in Wayfinding Strategies and Anxiety About Wayfinding: A Cross-Cultural Comparison." *Sex Roles: A Journal of Research,* Nov. 2002. Retrieved from http://findarticles.com/p/articles/mi_m2294/is_2002_Nov/ai_97728454.

Leahey, E. "Gender Differences in Mathematical Trajectories." *Social Forces,* 2001, *80,* 713–732.

Libby, M. N., & Aries, E. "Gender Differences in Preschool Children's Narrative Fantasy." *Psychology of Women Quarterly,* Sept. 1989, *13*(3), 203–306.

Luders, E., & others. "Gender differences in cortical complexity." *Nature Neuroscience,* 2000, *7,* 799–800.

McGinis, L., & others. "A Review of Gendered Consumption in Sport and Leisure." Retrieved from www.amsreview.org/articles/mcginnis05-2003.pdf.

McGivern, R. F., & others. "Gender Differences in Incidental Learning and Visual Recognition Memory: Support for a Sex Difference in Unconscious Environmental Awareness." *Personality and Individual Differences,* 1998, *25,* 223–232.

McKelvie, S. J., & others. "Gender Differences in Recognition Memory for Faces and Cars: Evidence for the Interest Hypothesis." *Bulletin of the Psychonomic Society,* 1993, *31*(5), 447–448.

Miller, K. "Gender Wars: Getting Boys and Girls to Play Together." *Parents.* Retrieved from www.parents.com/parents/story.jsp?storyid=/templatedata/parents/story/data/1150396041057.xml.

Multnomah County Library. *Brain Development: Birth to Six.* n.d. Retrieved from www.multcolib.org/birthtosix/braindev.html.

National Association for Same Sex Education. "What Are Some Differences in How Boys and Girls Learn?" Retrieved from www.singlesexschools.org.

The National Autistic Society. "Autism: Why Do More Boys Than Girls Develop It?" Retrieved from www.nas.org.uk/nas/jsp/polopoly.jsp?a=3370&d=1049.

National Institute of Neurological Disorders. "Autism Fact Sheet." Retrieved from www.ninds.nih.gov/disorders/autism/detail_autism.htm.

National Literacy Trust. "Talk to Your Baby: Gender and Language Development." Retrieved from www.literacytrust.org.uk/talktoyourbaby/gender.html.

NIMH. "Autism." Retrieved from www.nimh.nih.gov/health/publications/autism/complete-publication.shtml.

NIMH. "Attention Deficit Hyperactivity Disorder (ADHD)." Retrieved from www.nimh.nih.gov/health/topics/attention-deficit-hyperactivity-disorder-adhd/index.shtml .

Ostrov, J. M., & Keating, C. F. "Gender Differences in Preschool Aggression During Free Play and Structured Interactions: An Observational Study." *Social Development,* 2004, *13*(2), 255–277.

Rabinowicz, T., & others. "Structure of the Cerebral Cortex in Men and Women." *Journal of Neuropathology and Experimental Neurology,* Jan. 2002, *61*(1), 46–57.

"Research Summary—Gender in Education. Differences Between Boys and Girls." Learning About Learning. Retrieved from www.ltscotland.org.uk/learningaboutlearning/differences/research/rsgenderineducation.asp .

Rhoads, S. E. *Taking Sex Differences Seriously.* San Francisco: Encounter Books, 2004.

Robledo, S. J. "Developmental Milestone: Self-Care." *BabyCenter.* n.d. Retrieved from http://parentcenter.babycenter.com/0_developmental-milestone-self-care_63974.pc.

Sandstrom, N., Kaufman, J., & Huettel, S. A. "Males and Females Use Different Distal Cues in a Virtual Environment Navigation Task." *Cognitive Brain Research,* 1998, *6,* 351–360.

Saucier, D., & others. "Are Sex Differences in Navigation Caused by Sexually Dimorphic Strategies or by Differences in the Ability to Use the Strategies?" *Behavioral Neuroscience,* 2002, *116,* 403–410.

Schum, T., & others. "Sequential Acquisition of Toilet-Training Skills: A Descriptive Study of Gender and Age Differences in Normal Children." *Pediatrics,* Mar. 3, 2002, *109*(3), e48.

"Sex, Sexual Orientation and Sex Hormones Influence Human Cognitive Function." *Current Opinion in Neurobiology,* 1996, *6,* 259–263.

Shaywitz, B. A., & others. "Sex Differences in the Functional Organization of the Brain for Language." *Nature,* Feb. 16, 1995, *373,* 607–609.

Shechter, S., & others. "Gender Differences in Apparent Motion Perception." *Perception,* 1991, *20*(3), 307–314.

Sherar, L. B. "Age and Gender Differences in Youth Physical Activity: Does Physical Maturity Matter?" *Medicine and Science in Sports and Exercise,* 2007, *39*(5), 830–835.

"Structural Brain Variation and General Intelligence." *NeuroImage,* 2004, *23,* 425–433.

Sullivan, D. "Your 18-Month-Old's Social and Emotional Development: Making Friends." *BabyCenter.* n.d. Retrieved from www.babycenter.com/0_your-18-month-olds-social-and-emotional-development-making-f_1213792.bc.

Tannick, M. "Young Children's Rough and Tumble Play: Observations of Five Year Old Play." Retrieved from www.csuchico.edu/kine/tasp/06prespapers/tannockroughtumbleplaypaper.ppt.

Tchernigova, S. "Puzzling Boys and Girls: Gender Differences in Problem-Solving in Preschoolers Through Puzzles." 1995. Retrieved from www.eric.ed.gov/ERICDocs/data/ericdocs2sql/content_storage_01/0000019b/80/14/96/2a.pdf.

Thayer, J. F., & Johnsen, B. H. "Sex Differences in Judgment of Facial Affect: A Multivariate Analysis of Recognition Errors." *Scandinavian Journal of Psychology,* Sept. 2000, *41*(3), 243–246.

"Toddler's First Steps: A 'Best Chance' Guide to Parenting Your Six-Month- to Three-Year-Old." Retrieved from www.health.gov.bc.ca/cpa/publications/firststeps.pdf.

"Understanding and Raising Boys." PBS Parents. Retrieved from www.pbs.org/parents/raingboys/aggression02.html.

Vaughn, B. E., & others. "Negative Interactions and Social Competence for Preschool Children in Two Samples: Reconsidering the Interpretation of Aggressive Behavior for Young Children." *Merrill-Palmer Quarterly,* 2003, *49,* 518–521.

Weiman, H. "Gender Differences in Cognitive Functioning." Retrieved from http://homepages.luc.edu/~hweiman/GenderDiffs.html.

Willmer, J., & Nakayama, K. "A Large Gender Difference in Smooth Motion Pursuit." *Journal of Vision, 6*(6), Abstract 94, 94a.

Wilson, K. "Development of Conflicts and Conflict Resolution Among Preschool Children." *Canadian Journal of Education,* Winter 1997, *22*(1), 33–45.

"With Boys and Girls in Mind." *Educational Leadership.* Nov. 2004, *62*(3), 21–28.

Wood, G., & Shors, T. J. "Stress Facilitates Classical Conditioning in Males, But Impairs Classical Conditioning in Females Through Activational Effects of Ovarian Hormones." *Proceedings of the National Academy of Sciences,* 1998, *95,* 4066–4071.

Yark, F. "Gender Differences Are Real." *Narth.* Feb. 2008. Retrieved from www.narth.com/docs/york.html.

Chapter Four

Abrams, D. C. "The Making of a Modern Dad." *Psychology Today,* Mar. 2002, pp. 38–47.

Begley, S. "How Men and Women's Brains Differ." *Newsweek, 125*(3), 48.

Berg, S. J., & Wynne-Edwards, K. E. "Changes in Testosterone, Cortisol, and Estradiol Levels in Men Becoming Fathers." *Mayo Clinic Proceedings,* 2001, *76,* 582–592.

Blum, D. *Sex on the Brain: The Biological Differences Between Men and Women.* New York: Penguin Books, 1998.

Cahill, L. "Why Sex Matters for Neuroscience?" *Nature Reviews Neuroscience,* June 2006, *7,* 477–484.

Carey, B. "Men and Women Really Do Think Differently." *Live Science,* Jan. 20, 2005. Retrieved from www.livescience.com/health/050120_brain_sex.html.

Couzin, J. "A 'His' or 'Hers' Brain Structure." *Science Now Daily News,* Apr. 7, 2006.

Diamond, M. "Male and Female Brains: Lecture for Women's Forum." *West Annual Meeting,* San Francisco, Calif., 2003.

Eisler, R., & Levine, D. S. "Nurture, Nature and Caring: We Are Not Prisoners of Our Genes." *Brain and Mind,* 2002, *3,* 9–52.

Ellison, K. *The Mommy Brain: How Motherhood Makes Us Smarter.* New York: Basic Books, 2005.

Gray, P. B., & others. "Marriage and Fatherhood Associated with Lower Levels of Testosterone." *Evolution and Human Behavior,* 2002, 23, 193–201.

Gurian, M. *Nurture the Nature: Understanding and Supporting Your Child's Unique Core Personality.* San Francisco: Jossey-Bass, 2007.

Jovanovic, H. "PET Evaluation of Central Serotonergic Neuro-Transmission in Women." Doctoral thesis. Feb. 29, 2008. Retrieved from http://diss.kib.ki.se/2008/978-91-7357-510-2/thesis.pdf.

"Language and Gender: Women's Language and Men's Language." Retrieved from www.ldc.upenn.edu/myl/ling001/gender.htm.

LeVay, S. *The Sexual Brain.* Cambridge, Mass.: A Bradford Book, 1993.

Lemoick, M. "The Chemistry of Desire." *Time,* Jan. 12, 2004, 163(3), 68–72.

Marsa, L. "He Thinks, She Thinks." *Discover,* July 5, 2007. Retrieved from http://discovermagazine.com/2007/brain/she-thinks.

Moir, A., & Jessel, D. *Brain Sex: The Real Difference Between Men & Women.* New York: Dell, 1989.

Moir, A., & Moir, B. *Why Men Don't Iron.* New York: Citadel, 1999.

Mlyniec, V. "What a Son and a Daughter Need from a Mom." *Parents.com.* Retrieved from www.parents.com/parents/story.jsp?page=2&storyid=/templatedata/fc/story/data/1128972070434.xml.

Onion, A. "Sex in the Brain: Research Showing Men and Women Differ in More Than One Area." *ABC News,* Sept. 21, 2004.

Palmer, L. "Bonding Matters: The Chemistry of Attachment." *Attachment Parenting International News,* 2002, 5(2).

Pease, B., & Pease, A. *Why Men Don't Listen and Women Can't Read Maps.* New York: Broadway Books, 2000.

"Research in Gender and Brain Suggests Differences at Cell Level." *Society for Neuroscience,* Oct. 17, 2006. Retrieved from www.sfn.org/index.cfm?pagename=news_101706b

Sabbatini, R. "Are There Differences Between the Brains of Males and Females?" *Brain and Mind,* n.d. Retrieved from www.cerebromente.org.br/n11/mente/eisntein/cerebro-homens.html.

Schulz, M. L. *The New Feminine Brain.* New York: Free Press, 2005.

Sousa, D. A. *How the Brain Learns* (2nd ed.). Thousand Oaks, Calif.: Corwin Press, 2001.

Stossel, J. "Boys and Girls Are Different: Men, Women, and the Sex Difference." *ABC News Special,* Jan. 17, 1998, transcript from the Internet, The Electric Library.

Resources for Parents of Boys

In a world filled with constant input from the Internet and media, how does a parent choose what to read, view, or listen to?

We've done some preliminary filtering for you. Start here. You'll find further suggestions at these sites, or from your pediatrician, your friends, and family.

Book Ideas for Moms and Dads

The Wonder of Boys and *The Mind of Boys,* both by Michael Gurian.

The Dangerous Book for Boys, by Conn Iggulden and Hal Iggulden.

Raising a Son, by D. Elium and J. Elium.

What to Expect the First Year (2nd ed.), by Arlene Eisenberg.

T. Berry Brazelton, a noted pediatrician, has a number of books about infants, toddlers, sleep, and building a family. Two of his more recent publications include: *Touchpoints Birth to Three: Your Child's Emotional and Behavioral Development* and *The Irreducible Needs of Children: What Every Child Must Have to Grow.*

William Dougherty, family therapist, has written *The Intentional Family: Simple Rituals to Strengthen Family Ties,* a book that offers simple suggestions to build a family.

Help for Mothers of Boys

The Little Boy Book, by Sheila Moore and Roon Frost, Ballantine Books, 1987.

www.momsofboys.org is a wonderful Web site supporting mothers of boys.

Dad Support

Fatherhood, by Kyle Pruett. New York: Free Press, 2000.

The Literacy Trust Web site offers fathers assistance in how they can get involved in their sons' education. Find out more by going to www.literacytrust.org.uk.

Check out the October 2002 issue of *Parents Magazine* for an introduction to Fatherhood 101 in David Sparrow's article, "Bonding with Baby."

Help for Your Relationship

John Gottman has written several books applying biological research to relationships, including *Seven Principles for Making Marriages Work,* Three Rivers/Random House, 1999.

Also check out Michael Gurian's *What Could He Be Thinking?* St. Martins, 2004.

Why Talking Is Not Enough: Eight Loving Actions That Will Transform Your Marriage, by Susan Page. Jossey-Bass, 2007.

The Secrets of Happily Married Women: How to Get More Out of Your Relationship by Doing Less, by Scott Haltzman, MD, Theresa Foy DiGeronimo. Jossey-Bass, 2008.

The Secrets of Happily Married Men: Eight Ways to Win Your Wife's Heart Forever, by Scott Haltzman, MD, with Theresa Foy DiGeronimo. Jossey-Bass, 2007.

Books for Your Boy

Every year wonderful new books are published for toddlers and pre-schoolers. Here are a few where boy humor is often the topic.

The Truth About Poop, by Susan Goodman, Viking, 2004.

The Secret Science Project That Almost Ate the School, by Judy Sierra, Simon & Schuster, 2007.

Superdog: The Heart of a Hero, by Caralyn Buehner, HarperCollins, 2003.

Judith Viorst's books about her three real-life sons are classics. Our children loved *Alexander and the Terrible, Horrible, No Good, Very Bad Day,* Aladdin, 1997.

Other Classics Are:

Max's First Word, written and illustrated by Rosemary Wells, Dial, 1998, is the story of a small rabbit who outwits his bossy older sister as she insists on improving his vocabulary.

George and Martha, written and illustrated by James Marshall, Houghton Mifflin, 2008, features two plump hippos and the delicacy with which they respect each other's feelings.

Harry, the Dirty Dog, by Gene Zion, HarperTrophy, 1976, introduces us to Harry, a white dog with black spots, who buries the scrubbing brush to avoid his bath and sets forth on a series of adventures. He gets so dirty that he becomes a black dog with white spots and has to convince his family of his true identity.

The Story of Ferdinand, by Munro Leaf, Puffin, 2007, is about a peace-loving bull who prefers smelling flowers to fighting and is suddenly thrust into the bull ring with unexpected results.

Movies, TV, and Your Boy

Under age two, talking, singing, reading, listening to music, or playing are far more important to your son's development than any TV or movie. Brain research supports the American Academy of Pediatrics position that parents need to limit TV and movie viewing for toddlers and preschoolers. Be selective in choosing your son's first movies.

Before watching a movie with your preschooler check out the following site for advice on movies and your preschooler:

www.pbs.org/parents/childrenandmedia/tvmovies-preschool.html

And then enjoy a few of our favorites:

Bambi tells the coming-of-age story of a young buck who grows into a strong leader.

The Lion King follows a similar theme. Everyone loves to watch the young cub grow up and take over his pride.

Babe, the story of a young pig who herds sheep, gives boys the message that belief in oneself triumphs.

The Incredibles tells the story of some over-the-hill superheroes whose kids get to be superheroes in their own story. This is a favorite for both parent and child.

The Brave Little Toaster has a young boy hero rescuing his childhood love objects.

And once you tuck your boy in, grab a cup of tea and watch our favorite movie for moms and dads, *Parenthood* starring Steve Martin.

Support and Information on the Web

With hundreds of thousands of Internet sites devoted to parenting concerns, there's an overabundance of information available to you.

Following are a few suggestions to get you started:

The Gurian Institute assists parents in finding practical solutions to real life parenting dilemmas using the most recent scientific research. You can access the Institute at www.gurianinstitute.com. Parents may subscribe to the Institute's preschool newsletter for parents by clicking on the family link.

www.brainconnection.com provides cutting-edge information on brain development throughout the lifespan with particular attention devoted to education and problem solving.

PBS, a leading authority in children's television programming, presents a site dedicated to parenting. Parent guides to children's media, early math, and raising boys are available. You can find them at www.pbs.org/parents/issuesadvice.

A parent cooperative preschool is organized by a group of families with similar philosophies who hire a trained consultant/teacher. Parents gain insight into child behavior by observing other children. Children participate in a supervised play and learning experience with children of their own age, while parents and children develop an extended family with friendships they carry throughout their lives. Find out more about this built-in community at www.preschools.coop/home.htm

www.kidsindanger.com keeps parents current on product safety concerns.

www.kidshealth.org is an all-encompassing site that appeals to parents, kids, and teens, providing practical parenting information, homework help, teen advice, straight talk from professionals throughout the world, as well as doctor-approved health information about kids from birth through adolescence.

Information from the American Academy of Pediatrics can be found at www.aap.org.

If you have specific mental health concerns about your son, consult:

www.ncld.org, a site which provides parents with information about learning disabilities, their warning signs, and resources to contact.

The Web site for the National Institute of Mental Health found at www.nimh.nih.gov/health also has information on both autism and hyperactivity.

The Gurian Institute

If you would like to help your community better meet the developmental needs of both boys and girls, please contact the Gurian Institute. The Institute works with parents, schools, business corporations, the juvenile and adult corrections systems, medical and mental health professionals, and others who serve children and adults.

Gurian Institute staff and trainers provide training and regional conferences, working throughout the United States, as well as in Canada and abroad. The Institute provides resources and services through four divisions: Families, Education, Corporate, and Human Services. Each can be accessed through www.gurianinstitute.com.

The Institute is committed to providing both science-based information and practical and relevant applications for everyday life. We help build self-sufficiency in communities. We believe that alone, each parent and each professional is a visionary; at the same time, by working together, we become the protective and successful social force our children and families most need.

To learn more, please visit www.gurianinstitute.com.

About the Authors

Stacie Bering, MD, is a board-certified obstetrician-gynecologist who practiced and taught obstetrics and gynecology for twenty-five years in Spokane, Washington. Health issues led to her second board certification in hospice and palliative medicine. She is now the medical director of an inpatient palliative medicine service for Empire Health Services in Spokane. She shares her precious free time skiing and traveling with her husband, Jeffry, and grown children Cassie and Zack in Spokane.

Adie Goldberg, ACSW, MEd, is a board-certified social worker who has worked in many clinical and university settings. She has been a psychiatric social worker at WomanHealth, an OB-GYN practice, for twenty years. This collaborative medical–social work practice model has received national attention. Eight years ago she began working as a Jewish education director at Temple Beth Shalom, and as part of this work, became a certified Gurian Institute Trainer. She utilizes gender brain concepts in both educational and clinical settings. Adie presents at local and national conventions on a broad range of topics and writes for both social work and Jewish journals on family, education, and spirituality issues. She is almost an empty nester with two adult daughters, Emily and Maggie, and a third daughter, Chloe, who is in high school. Adie can be reached at www. gurianinstitute.com.

Index